Meny Chri~
Geo~
May the Beasties
always be at your
side!
Love,
Sarah

D1111522

"Nature is an unlimited broadcasting station,
through which [the universe] speaks
to us every hour, if only we will tune in."

George Washington Carver

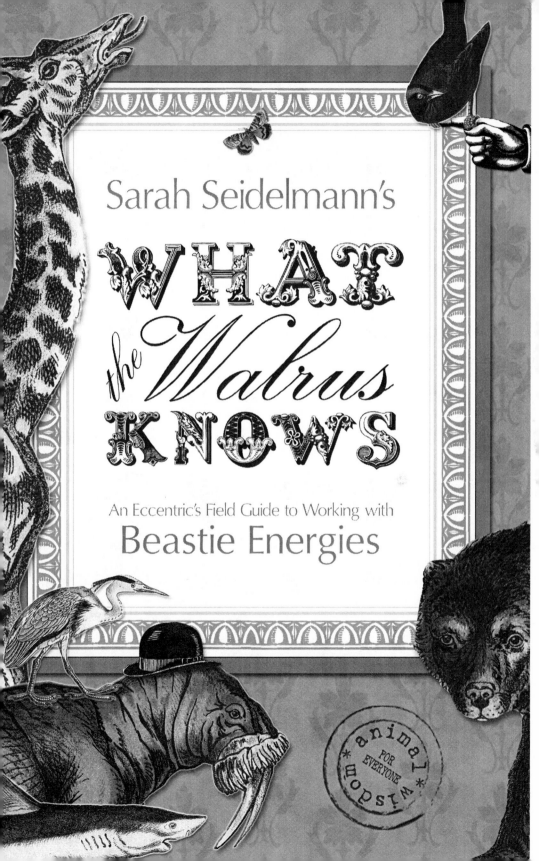

Sarah Seidelmann's

WHAT the Walrus KNOWS

An Eccentric's Field Guide to Working with
Beastie Energies

animal wisdom
FOR EVERYONE

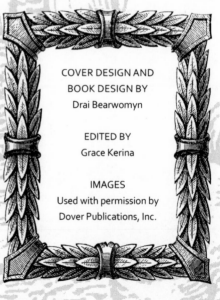

THANKS!

This book is dedicated to all the wild
and beautiful Beasties. **THANK YOU**
for sharing your fantasticness with me.

And to my family and closely-knit
circle of lovely honey badgers, who
love me and **INSPIRE ME** daily.

INTRODUCTION

BEASTIE: Any insect, reptile, bird, mammal, or mythical creature that exists or has ever existed, from salmon to woolly mammoths to dragonflies.

Introduction

A while ago, I fell madly in love with a taxidermied walrus. I couldn't stop myself from going back to the little shop a block from my office where he lived. At the time, I was a bit wild about money and how I'd replace the income I'd lose if I left my job as a physician. My aim was to be more free to pursue what I loved, but so far I was just worried.

I'd been living a nature-starved, over-civilized life for a long time. My husband and I are both physicians, and we're raising four kids. Add all my other interests to the mix, and the result was a constant state of overwhelm. I was on sabbatical from my work as a pathologist, though I continued to do my life-coaching work with clients. As I started spending more time in nature, taking more walks and noticing what was happening around me, I began to feel better. Then I picked up *Animal Speak*, Ted Andrews' book on animal totems, and began my journey into a magical world.

When I became aware that Beasties might have something to teach me, my whole life cracked open.

I found that connecting with Mr. Walrus and the spirit I sensed in him (even in his taxidermied state) felt deeply reassuring. I discovered that the walrus is a powerful Beastie, offering strength, abundance, gregariousness, deep diving, and even a touch of the psychic. To this day, whenever I think of that walrus, a feeling of deep security comes over me.

MAGICAL SUPPORT AND LOVE SURROUNDED ME.

Many amazing things began to happen in rapid sequence. I attracted an insanely fabulous opportunity to travel to Africa, I realized it was time for me to step away from my medical job altogether, and I manifested the money to make all of that possible and easy. But the most important thing was that I found a deep sense of peace and joy through discovering what Beasties had to teach me, which I would love for you to find as well.

Because of the connections I made with Beasties and nature, I had an awakening. I began to have a sense of magical support and love surrounding me. During my sabbatical, my resistance to what I wanted decreased dramatically. I suddenly felt connected, like I belong to this world. I began to see beauty everywhere and experienced many moments of ecstatic joy. I entered a joyful, peaceful state of harmony that had previously eluded me. As a result of making this connection with nature, I've felt real magic in my life. That's why I'm passionate about sharing it.

This not a guide to help you *identify* Beasties, but to help you identify *with* Beasties. Identifying with Beasties happens not in a linear left-brain way, but in an intuitive right-brain way, beneath the surface.

My true heart's desire is to tell you about Beasties and their energies in a way that's fun and easy to understand, so you can discover their power and joy for yourself.

Appreciation

There's a bigger, deeper world all around us all the time, full of messages and support. We're marinating in it. It permeates and surrounds our ordinary reality. I wasn't aware of this deeper world until the Beastie spirits (energies) seemed to find me and I started connecting with them. Observing Beasties helps us tap into this deeper level of information.

Connecting with Beasties is an empowering way to invite personal transformation and to manifest what we want. Many of us (especially me) tend to get stuck in our heads. We try to solve the problems of our lives using our left-brain linear intellect. Often, though, those of us who are "left-hefty" need to get out of that mode in order to manifest change more effortlessly.

One of the fastest and most magical ways to manifest change is through appreciation, which connects us to intuitive knowledge. Our divine self knows what's possible for us and knows the easiest ways to get things done. The ancients knew this, too.

We tap into appreciation more easily when we're in nature or observing the natural world. If you're familiar with the teachings of Buddhism or yoga or Eckhart Tolle, you've likely come across the idea that in a state of appreciation, joy and expanded possibilities are more available to us because we're not concerned about the past or worried about the future. We're just here in this moment, appreciating our now.

Ask people how they get themselves into a really good-feeling place and they'll tell you things like they listen to music they love, or look at a great piece of art, or connect with a friend or loved one. They also say they go outside. Being in nature is a great way to feel good. We walk dogs, stroll along beaches, take hikes, sit on benches in parks ... and feel better. One of my favorite clients floats in the water on a little raft. However we do it, being in nature opens us and helps us connect to what's bigger than we are. It lifts our vibration.

When we spend time in nature, we rekindle our primal connection with the earth. That's why the sounds of nature — the crash of waves, the hum of rain, wind in the trees — are very grounding and reassuring. We're tuning in to Mother Earth, one of the most powerful manifestors of all.

You don't need to move out into the wilderness or set up camp in a yurt to experience this wonderful earth connection. You can do it from wherever you are right now. Whether you live in Los Angeles or Chicago, in the middle of the desert, or anywhere else, it's a wonderful place to begin. You only need a little curiosity.

Like Attracts Like

The Law of Attraction is the concept that like attracts like — something with a certain vibration attracts other things with a similar vibration. The idea is that if we spend a lot of time in a certain state, we'll attract into our lives more experiences, people, things, and events that match that state. If we're frustrated, we'll attract more frustration. If we're joyful, we'll attract more joy.

From a shamanic perspective, everything is alive, infused with conscious energy or spirit, and interconnected. Quantum physics increasingly seems to offer evidence of this concept, too, with its theories of entanglement and the idea that adding an observer appears to change the behavior of subatomic particles.

The way this ties in with Beastie energies is that everything has a vibration — some would call it spirit — including all natural things, like rocks, flowers, trees, insects, birds, and mammals — and that the vibrations of things in nature are inherently high and positive. They're very powerful manifestors because they don't experience a lot of resistance to their own selves. As Deepak Chopra says, "The grass doesn't try to grow. It just grows." Beasties are not judgmental or resistant to their own existence the way humans often are. The walrus doesn't say, "Oh, good heavens! I'm getting so fat! Why do I lay here for hours in the sun at the beach with my friends? I should be exercising more or starting that diet or catching up on my emails instead." No. The walrus knows that all is well. It's doing what it loves and enjoys. It's following its instincts without getting into its head too much.

When Beasties shows up in our experience, it's like an invitation to join in their vibration. Wild Beasties are radically self-loving – they're vibrational role models, in a way. When we're able to love and accept ourselves, there's really no other work to be done. We experience joy and abundance. Becoming aware of Beasties can help us find that place in ourselves.

I believe that when we connect and align with self-love and self-acceptance and harness that to left-brain intellect, there's nothing we can't do or create. This is powerful stuff.

By being curious about what's around us and simply noticing the Beasties that show up in our lives, we connect with their higher vibrations and discover all sorts of things about ourselves and how to positively manifest what we want.

An Ancient Practice

Working with Beastie spirits is an ancient practice that's been going on for tens of thousands of years on every continent. Most of us weren't raised in the Amazon Basin surrounded by shamans. Most of us have long forgotten how to tune in to nature's information and assistance because we've been raised in a culture where humans believe that we're somehow superior to the rest of the natural world in terms of intelligence and abilities. Why would we want to tune in to something we believe to be inferior and not as powerful as we are, like an ant? We're coming to realize, even through hard sciences that look at issues like biodiversity and habitat, that every creature's contributions are critical for the health of all.

The wonderful thing is that it's not too late. You can benefit from the natural world right away, simply by beginning to work with it. Many times, I've witnessed how quickly and easily this connection becomes a natural part of people's lives as they open to it and sense it all around.

I think there's something ancient embedded in our DNA or our collective experience about working with nature and Beasties. We still see signs of this connection in our most modern creations. In the movie *Avatar*, for example, the hero connects with horse energy. When he's about to ride the horse for the first time, he takes the end of his own braid and connects it to the end of the horse's tail. At first it's awkward – and sometimes it can be that way with learning to connect to Beastie energies – but once the bond is made and their energies are shared, the hero is able to ride to many wonderful places and do many things he wouldn't have been able to do without sharing power and energy with the horse.

The process of working with Beasties and natural energies is like plugging into the endless power source of Mother Earth. It's like having direct access to a gigantic, infinitely powerful charging station.

It's NOT too late...

Tune In to Totems

A *totem* is any natural object – it could be a Beastie (insect, reptile, bird, mammal, or extinct or mythical Beastie), a plant, a rock, or even a planet – that bears a special significance for an individual. A totem is a source of strength and insight that the person would not have without it. Another way of saying this is that a totem's vibrational energy is aligned with the person using that totem. The more you honor and consult with a totem, the more strongly aligned and higher your own vibration will become.

There are two basic kinds of Beastie totems. The first I like to think of as **Guest Beasties**. They're around for a limited time. They come to stay with us for a moment or a month, or even a year, to bring a message or share some wisdom. Guest Beasties arrive to guide us through something important that's going on in our life. They're basically saying, "Hey! Over here! Notice me, because I'm trying to tell you something that's important for you to know."

Guest Beasties may come to you when you're outdoors, whether in the woods or on the way out to the car. But there are many other ways they come to us, and they all count. They may come into your awareness through a television or computer screen. Someone may give you a card with a cartoon of a Beastie on it. Maybe you see a carving of a Beastie in a museum, or a logo on a shirt as you're doing the laundry. Just by paying attention to what shows up in your awareness you can begin to tune in to these Guest Beasties.

The other kind of beastie we'll explore is what I like to think of as **Core Beasties**. Other writers refer to them as guardians, power animals, or protectors. As I began to teach and share

I only went out for a walk and finally concluded to stay out till sundown, for going out, I found, was really going in.

John Muir

Beastie knowledge with others, the word "power" often seemed to be thought of only as "intimidation" and "strength." While it's true that a Core Beastie does offer strength, it's not the strength of being more powerful than others, but the strength that comes from being connected to your own self. The "Core" in "Core Beastie" is the core of YOU.

Core Beasties stay with us for many, many years – often for a lifetime. They're usually a wild Beastie and they're often a mammal, probably because we humans are mammals, so they're most closely related to us. A Core Beastie is very protective and empowering. Having a Core Beastie is like having a wonderful mentor alongside for a lifetime.

Before we go further, let's talk about pets. People often ask, "Can I do this Beastie energies work with my pet?" Sure. It's a great way to start, particularly if you struggle with connecting to wild Beasties. Domesticated Beasties are in service to humans in some way, whereas a wild Beastie lives outside that impact of human vibrations. So, know that even though you can use a pet as a way into working with Beastie totems, wild Beasties may offer you an even more powerful connection to positive vibrations.

Begin with Three Steps

Beginning to work with Beasties requires almost no effort at all.

The first step is simply to notice what Beasties show up as you go about your day – as you read the newspaper or watch TV, as you pick up the mail or walk down the street. Even notice mythical or extinct beasts, like unicorns, dragons, or dinosaurs, as the principles for working with them are the same.

As you notice what Beasties are showing up, also notice what they're doing. *What activity are they involved in? Are they flying, sleeping, hunting, or snuggling?* Simply notice.

The second step is to notice what's on your mind when the Beastie enters your awareness. Are you thinking about an issue you're having with a business associate? Are you mulling over a big step you're thinking of taking? Are you reviewing an incident with a friend? Or thinking about a relationship that needs healing? Again, simply notice.

The third step is to look in a book or on the Internet to find out more about the Beastie you noticed. Explore the animal in a way that feels good to you. Then ask yourself: *What insights does this exploration reveal or evoke in me regarding what's on my mind?* What instant "Aha!" do you get, if any? If nothing rises to the surface ... simply be patient and wait. Often, a significant insight will occur to you later.

You can use the Beastie Manifestos provided in this book to explore some of their special qualities and attitudes, to explore some of the ways their energies may show up in your life. The manifestos have been inspired by my own experiences, while working with my clients, and by the hours I've spent on *Squirrel! Radio* interacting with brilliant people, listening to their stories, and learning about the ways they've experienced these Beasties.

If you can't find a Beastie in the manifestos, don't be dismayed. There's a resource guide at the end of the book to help you find the odd Beastie not listed here. My goal with this field guide is to provide you with a hearty collection of Beastie Manifestos, in the hope that you'll find one or several you feel a connection with. I've also thrown in a few odd and special Beasties that have been particularly powerful for me.

As you read about the Beastie, think about what you noticed about the Beastie itself, what it was doing, and about what you were thinking about at the time. Interpretations of Beastie energies and spirits that others write can be very helpful, but the most powerful messages and connections you'll make as you go about your interpretation are the ones that will begin to come from within you. You may find that your internal knowing about what a Beastie signifies when it comes into your awareness will be the most meaningful.

Intention

Setting an intention is a powerful thing. What would you like to happen as you explore the world around you and the Beastie Manifestos? What would you like to happen today? How would you like the Universe to shift? Clear intentions help us shift and lift our vibrations, and make the connections that are all around us all the time easier to see.

**My intention is to help you discover
something powerful about yourself today.**

The next two chapters cover Guest Beasties and Core Beasties. The remainder of the book is a compilation of Beastie Manifestos, which you can use like a field guide to help you discover more about Beasties and how they can help.

GUEST BEASTIES

"What is life. It is the flash of the firefly at night and it is the breath of the Buffalo in the wintertime. It is the little shadow that runs across the grass and loses itself in the sunset."

Blackfoot

Guest Beasties   NO SHEET CHANGING REQUIRED!

Even our biggest fears, like not having enough money or love, or having poor health, can be powerfully healed by connecting with the message or wisdom of a Beastie. I know it sounds wacky, but give it a try. You really don't need to be in a wilderness area, although being in nature will definitely facilitate the process. You don't even need to be in the geographic area where the living Beastie makes it's home to experience the power of Guest Beasties. Just begin where you are right now.

Invite Guest Beasties to Visit

In the introduction, I explained a three-step process for starting to work with Beasties. That's the process for working with Guest Beasties, which are Beasties that appear for a limited time to bring you a specific message. It's kind of like a guest coming to stay in your home for a while to point you in a new direction or teach you something. But you don't have to change the sheets or wake up to make sure the coffee is on (my favorite kind of guest!).

Here's an example of how a Guest Beastie might appear. When I first started sharing this idea of the Beasties offering us guidance, I had a discussion about it with a dear friend. Afterward, he went to a café and sat with a hot tea in a to-go cup, waiting until it was cool enough to drink. It had been a rather brutal morning. His wife had been served papers for a lawsuit, which was surprising and upsetting. On top of that, he and his family had recently left their church to begin a new life more in alignment with their values, so they were beginning from scratch to build a new community. He lifted the lid on his tea and took a sip just as he noticed there'd been a fly trapped under the lid. He swallowed the fly down with the tea before he could stop himself.

Our conversation about Beastie totems was still on his mind, so he thought, *You know, normally I'd be grossed out right now. But maybe there's a message here.* He went home and looked up the fly totem. In the particular reference he used, this passage stood out: "This is a time of rapid abundance growing." It went on to say that in a short period – two weeks or so – abundance would show up. He connected with that possibility. It felt true and reassuring. That little fly helped him raise his vibration that morning, connecting to hope and anticipation *despite* his circumstances. It turned out that many good things did come his way as a result of his wife's lawsuit. They began to reach out for a new community and found one that continues to grow. Also, though the lawsuit was stressful, it brought them closer together as they supported each other.

Often, a Beastie will show up just for a moment to remind us that all will be well. Feeling good (or at least a bit better) in the moment is sometimes all we can do to change our situation. Finding that relief when it seems everything is falling apart can be so reassuring.

Get in the Flow by Looking for Signs

The power of connecting with messages from Beasties is that they reconnect us to the all-knowing part of ourselves, the divine part that knows *all is well* and *all will be well.* This can help us relax and get into the flow of life and stop swimming upstream. There's often an intuitive connection that's made while studying totems and their meanings. If you consider Guest Beasties to be symbols, as totems are, it can be easier to

tap into your right brain's ability to notice and use metaphor and intuition to interpret their messages. Daniel Pink, in his book *A Whole New Mind*, says tapping into the right brain is critical for thriving in the new economy. Using both logic and intuition is powerful, whether you're building a business, raising a child, or changing the world in your own unique way.

If you've ever read about or experienced the power of interpreting dream messages, you already know that working with symbols is powerful. An example is that the life cycle of the Beastie that brings a messages can be symbolic. A Beastie's life cycle or reproductive cycle can be part of a message about how much time it may take for abundance to appear or for the manifestation of a creative project. A fly, for instance, reproduces quite quickly, so it can be a symbol for abundance and quick renewal. In contrast, elephants have a very long gestational period, so elephants are showing up everywhere as you work on a project it could mean that it's going to take longer than a few short weeks to make it happen.

Beasties can symbolize and mirror qualities we ourselves have or seek. A taxidermied walrus (odd, I know) drew me toward it and toward its strength and power, which helped me find my own strength and power. That fly showed my friend a way to feelings of relief, which helped him manifest the changes he wanted. When we're open to connections between what we want and need and what Beasties show us, we can discover so much about ourselves and our lives.

Follow Your Feel Good

There are so many fun ways to play with Guest Beasties and to think about them. Whatever feels good to you as a way to work

    sarah bamford seidelmann m.d. | www.whatthewalrusknows.com

with Beastie totems is the right way for you. Be open to the possibilities and to ways of noticing that feel good to explore.

Sometimes a Guest Beastie will show up, we'll read about the totem, and *we'll think, That makes no sense or I don't like the message I'm getting from that.* That's okay. There's no need to push. There's no need to try to make sense of it. We can let it unfold. More may be revealed later.

Oftentimes, I won't understand a Guest Beastie message on the day I receive it, but a couple of days later it'll all become clear. Sometimes I resist a message. I don't worry about it. If it's a message I'm supposed to get, it'll show up again later. The Beasties are quite patient. If the message rings true or resonates, fabulous! Say a little thank you to your Guest Beastie and apply its message in your life.

It can be powerful to keep a little notebook handy and write down what's showing up and what possible totem readings might be. Then you can start to learn more about yourself and ways that work for you to explore Guest Beasties. It's also great to record this stuff if you're feeling skeptical. Beasties don't mind skeptics at all! You can check back and see if the messages you received became helpful over time. As you notice patterns and themes, they can help you see a bigger picture. The accumulation of messages and meanings can show you how you can make your own life as fabulous as it can be. You can begin to see your own dreams coming true as you explore and track what Guest Beasties tell you.

Beasties Showing Up

You don't need to see a Beastie in three dimensions for it to be a Guest Beastie with a message for you. Beasties you see on TV, in movies, on a gift someone gives you – they all count. You may even hear a Beastie rather than see it. Or you might see a tail, a tooth, a glistening trail on the sidewalk, a web, scat, or other evidence of the Beastie. Ask yourself, *How does the WAY in which I'm seeing this Beastie – or the part of it that it has left for me to see – make sense in the context of what's on my mind?*

Where a Guest Beastie appears can be part of its message. Ask yourself, *Where is this message showing up?* If you're at home, it might be in the front yard, which is a public area we project to the world, or it might be in the backyard, perhaps representing a more private part of you. Or is it showing up on your commute to work? Just be curious.

Let Go of Resistance

Wonderful solutions come up when we stop resisting and play. Using Guest Beastie energy can be super simple and great fun to play around with.

A woman who's an industrial psychologist was starting to enjoy exploring totems. One day, she was driving down a road through the woods and saw hundreds of geese in a pond. They all had their beaks down in the water. She asked herself, *Okay, what's the significance of this?* She remembered that I'd suggested she notice what they were doing and also what was on her mind. As she did that, she started to laugh. "Oh my gosh!" she told me later. "I knew exactly what they were doing! They were all mooning me because on that particular day I really needed a good laugh."

Ask Yourself Questions

A professional singer told me about being in a time of great distress. She went on a walk and ended up sitting by an inland lake. As she was thinking about not knowing quite what to do about everything she was facing, a single dragonfly showed up and buzzed around her. For about an hour it never strayed more than a few feet away. She thought, *Gosh, I don't even really need to know the specific significance of the dragonfly Beastie message because I have such a feeling of protection from it right now – and of company and a presence that's with me during a time when I really need it.*

Exploring what the appearance of a Guest Beastie means may be as simple as it was for the woman with the dragonfly – you don't even need to read about the totem specifically. You can just ask yourself, *What feeling do I get from this Beastie showing up right now?* Quick! What's that flash of insight – some call it an intuitive hit – that pops up. Pay attention to it before the logical, linear mind jumps in to squash or edit it.

Common and Uncommon Beasties

Some Guest Beasties will seem very rare and unusual, and some will seem quite common. You may wonder if that means anything. For starters, read about the Beasties you're drawn to. That's why the taxidermied walrus was perfect for starting me on my explorations – he was very foreign and yet he had a powerful message for me. I've noticed that some people begin most successfully with the Beasties that constantly congregate on their lawn at home. You cannot make a wrong turn with Beasties. Just begin.

If you're feeling resistance to a Guest Beastie, like you can't imagine it could have any significance for you, then don't push it. Start with something easier or more appealing instead.

People often ask me things like, "You know, there are always a bunch of crows cawing in my yard. Is that significant? Should I begin there?" I say that if you notice a Beastie, there's definitely something there for you. But, again, don't push it. Look at what you're drawn to. Over time, the scope of your interest in the kinds of Guest Beasties that come calling may expand.

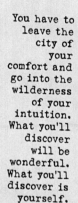

Beastie Equal Rights

People frequently ask me this question: "What if it's an icky Beastie or a Beastie I don't like that shows up?" I've learned that there are a few Beasties that often scare people – snakes, spiders, and sharks, to name a few. It's important to remember that all Beasties – from ants to lions – have their own special significance, power, and strength. In nature, there's no judgment that the lion is better than the ant or the hyena is worth less than the salmon.

In our culture, we tell a lot of stories that put judgments on certain Beasties – through movies, for example. Humans often judge certain Beasties as bad (spiders and jackals) and others as good (swans and butterflies), but in the natural world there is no judgment. Each Beastie plays an incredibly powerful and important role. Without each of those Beasties playing their part, the entire web of life suffers. We're all connected. It's good to consider ourselves and all the Beasties as equal parts of that web.

The idea that every Beastie is equally important in the web of life correlates well to the idea that every human is equally as important as every other human, that we're each here for a specific purpose and mission and none of us is more or less powerful than the other. It's my belief that things work best if we all share our specific gifts, choosing how we express our purpose here on Earth and the strengths we've been given. Just as each Beastie was put here to do its special thing, *you* were put here to rock your unique self and your talents.

Beastie Fears

If a Beastie that you're scared of shows up, like maybe a spider or snake, then learning a little bit more about them can be a powerful way of connecting with its vibration and letting go of some of that resistance and fear. Something to keep in mind is that when we learn more about a Beastie, we also learn more about ourselves. As we do this work with Beasties, we become more conscious and our awareness is raised.

On *Squirrel! Radio*, where we talk about Beasties and their messages on a regular basis, we had a caller who told us she'd been in her kitchen one day about to take a napkin and squish a spider she saw on the floor – something she'd done hundreds of times before – but as she was leaning over to do it, she stopped, because she realized that the spider might have a message for her. She felt so happy and pleased with herself because she'd shifted to thinking of the spider as a Guest Beastie. This is an example of the big shift in consciousness that happens as we do this work. She read about what the spider had to offer her and felt even better and more connected. In fact, she felt fantastic. She was able to cherish the spider's message and power and special gifts.

When we can do this – honor Guest Beasties – it shows us that we've learned to honor our own messages, that we're willing to honor our own desires and yearnings. Opening in this way to the messages of all Beasties that come into our lives is a method of cultivating self-love. That may sound freaky to you if you're a spider-hater now, yet I've witnessed that transition time and time again with clients and callers to our radio program and many of the people I speak with about this Beasties work. When you start paying attention and being curious, everything changes.

Nature in general can be a mirror for us. We begin to see more beauty, power, strength, and everything else reflected back to us as we grow in our own belief that we ourselves are beautiful and powerful.

BEASTIES ARE SIMPLY GOING ABOUT THEIR WORK...

Beastie Energies

People ask me, "Don't some Beasties have bad energy?" and "Aren't some Beasties evil?" My answer is, "No." This kind of thinking may go back to superstitious beliefs and judgments that have been placed on certain Beasties by other cultures or religions or by the media. Beasties are simply going about their work, which is to fully express themselves and their talents here on Earth. If we're having difficulty understanding or relating to them, then taking the time to learn a bit more about a Beastie can help us understand their behavior and their meaning in our lives. Or ... skip the Beasties you're concerned about, for now, and spend time with ones you're more easily attracted to.

It's only in recent history that we humans have placed ourselves at the top of the so-called "Ladder of Beasts." Our view of our intellectual prowess put us in the "King of the World" slot at the top. In ancient times, when we lived much closer to the natural world, Beasties were often put above humans in terms of

sarah bamford seidelmann m.d. | www.whatthewalrusknows.com

power, intelligence, and wisdom. When the influential psychiatrist Carl Jung traveled in Africa, he noticed that the indigenous people he spent time with there put the elephant and the crocodile above humans in terms of wisdom and power.

In fact, Beasties are incredible. They can do things humans can't. Birds fly. A tiger can run 35 miles an hour. A spider can weave a web that's miles long, with an amazing tensile strength compared to its delicate appearance. The hefty and weighty bumblebee flies in a way that, from a physics point of view (that darn logic!), shouldn't work – but it does. No one Beastie or human is more powerful than any other. And since we're all interconnected, this web is stronger when each of us contributes a part of ourselves to it. Our connections within the web make us stronger, too. In other words, as the bee defies gravity, so do you.

By connecting to the messages Beasties of all kinds bring to us, we can access hidden information we wouldn't normally have access to. That's part of the magic of opening ourselves to Guest Beasties.

Powerful Connections

When you're interpreting messages from the Beasties, it's powerful to filter the interpretation through your core beliefs and your sense of what's true for you. That's what distinguishes this work with Beasties from silly superstition. Check out possible interpretations or guidance with your own gut, or run it through your "Does this make sense ?" filter. That's where success comes from: consistently using your intuitive senses (right brain or spirit) in concert with your logic and intelligence (left brain and groundedness).

Sometimes, going within and contemplating the Beastie and the context and what you're thinking about can be very powerful. You may get a simple, straightforward message that immediately means something to you, or a little input from an outside source can spark a deeper connection.

I was in South Africa with a dear friend who was absolutely terrified of monkeys. For years, she'd been saying to her friends, "I hate two things: monkeys and clowns." As we boarded the plane for South Africa, she said, "I can't wait to get there, but I'm scared to death about the monkeys."

One morning in South Africa, as we were sitting at a table on the outdoor patio of a beautiful lodge at a gorgeous preserve, enjoying watching the animals and birds, a huge male baboon – about five feet tall, we later learned – jumped off the roof, landed on the breakfast buffet, knocked some gigantic pots off the table, and made a general ruckus. Then he bounced off the table and started running straight for us. It was pretty terrifying. He was BIG. Just before he got to our table, he was chased off by some of the staff, who whapped him with a walnut they shot out of a slingshot.

It had been a scary few moments and my friend was very, very upset. She tried to catch her breath. Finally, she said, "I need to go back to the room and rest. That was too much." All of a sudden, a beautiful white crane flew over us, gliding through the air. She said, "Uh oh. We'd better look that up in our totem book." Through the chaos and stress she began to be curious about what the significance of the crane was. We looked in Ted Andrews' *Animal-Speak Pocket Guide* and found this: "Crane ... Spiritual justice at play. Karma will be playing out somewhere in your life. Reflect on past lives and past issues." She started to laugh, because it was karma. For 20 years she'd been telling people how much she hated monkeys.

The input from the crane shifted my friend's perspective about baboons. An internal shift was made by reading about the crane totem and applying that to her experience. I watched as her complete distress and upset were transformed into laughter. She knew she still had more work to do, yet the shift was powerful and uplifting. This is what Beasties can do for us.

Early on in my explorations about Beasties, I asked for a dream to show me a sign of a Core Beastie (the next chapter is about Core Beasties). Lo and behold, a black mamba snake showed up. Good grief! I didn't want a snake for a Core Beastie, especially a poisonous one. Over time, though, I re-explored the idea and did a lot of interacting, via shamanic journeying, with the lovely black mamba snake. As it turns out, the snake was there to ask me to let go of old patterns and be willing to get up and dance.

So if you're resisting a Beastie that's showing up, as I was, it's all good. There's probably a powerful message in there for you, yet there's no rush to figure it out or to face it. If you choose to, however, you may be very pleasantly surprised.

...IT'S ALL GOOD.

Beastie Synchronicities

I and many of my clients and others who work with Beasties have discovered that there are often big synchronicities at play in the messages of Guest Beasties.

A fellow physician and I were sitting outside having lunch at a beautiful restaurant in the woods and saw five skunks – a mother and four babies – walk across an expanse of grass. Just prior to seeing the skunks, we'd been talking intensely about some issues my friend was having with her chemically addicted father. I was also struggling with issues around putting up boundaries with coaching clients by phone and being able to respect my own time. Our sighting of skunks in broad daylight felt unusual to me and begged for further investigation.

That night, I read more about skunks. Skunks know how to put up boundaries with brilliance. They raise their tail as a warning and if you come too close to their personal space they will spray you. Aha! This skunk Guest Beastie message seemed to be telling me that I needed to put up boundaries in my own way, that nobody could do it for me. How might I metaphorically "put up my tail" as a warning that I had only 20 minutes to talk on the phone with a prospective client before I needed to go tend to the other projects I also loved?

Another example of Beastie synchronicity happened one night when my husband and I were driving home and three raccoons crossed the road in front of our car. Earlier that evening, we'd talked extensively about my six-month sabbatical from my medical job and whether I'd eventually go back to work or not. We were wondering what the right decision might be.

When we got home, I read about the raccoon totem and found out that raccoons have a 20-week gestation cycle from conception to giving birth. Also, the masked face of the raccoon suggested that I was pretending to be something I'm not or that I was wearing some kind of mask. The source I read suggested that in about 20 weeks my mask might be dropped. I looked at a calendar and saw that if I went back to my medical job, I'd do so in exactly 20 weeks. Hmmm. At that moment, I didn't know what my decision was going to be, but I felt relieved to know I'd be dropping a mask of some kind. Wearing a mask – pretending to be someone you're not – is exhausting. It smacked of truth that in 20 weeks I'd be dropping a mask, either by not going back to pathology or by being much more open at work about also pursuing my coaching career. I wasn't yet sure which it would be, but I felt a strong synchronicity between my life and the message from the raccoons.

By the time I reached the end of those 20 weeks, I'd decided to drop my mask altogether. I didn't return to my medical job, but continued to fully pursue the true love of my life: coaching, connecting, speaking, and inspiring others to step into their own fantastic light.

Explore More

So, as you may have seen for yourself by now, Beasties are continually showing up for us and offering the possibility of insights, clues, and hints. I find that these fabulous Beasties often provide me with information that talking with a friend, reading a self-help book, or meditating on a lotus would not have.

I invite you to simply notice what Beasties show up for you today. If you're irrepressible, like I am, when you notice a Beastie, quickly flip over to the Beastie Manifestos section in this book and read to see if your meeting smells like truth in some way. If you haven't noticed any Beasties yet today, set an intention to see one Guest Beastie before you go to sleep tonight. Just see what happens.

Play around for a while. Explore the meanings of the Guest Beasties that come into your awareness. See what comes up for you.

Up next is discovering your Core Beastie –

a very special Beastie that's probably been with you all along.

CORE BEASTIES
- DIVING IN -

"A connection with a Core Beastie - what some people call a power animal - can be one of the most magical relationships, mentorships, and friendships you'll ever have. That's what it's been for me, and what I hope it'll be for you, too." SBS

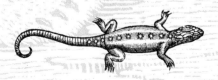

Core Beasties – Diving In

I chose the name "Core Beastie" because I believe it more clearly communicates what this relationship is about. Besides, it's my nature to see things a little differently. I love that about me.

Some people call Core Beasties "power animals," but the word "power" is often confusing. The Core Beastie you connect with will empower you – yet it isn't power as our culture tends to popularly define it: the ability to dominate the world or control others. The power I'm talking about here is the quiet strength that comes from being and expressing your unique essence in all the realms of your life.

A Core Beastie is an animal you have a relationship with over a very long period of time. Many experts on this topic say that a Core Beastie is often with you for your entire lifetime.

Let's explore how to discover your Core Beastie.

Core Beastie Basics

If you've been experimenting with what it's like to work with Guest Beasties, you've been priming the pump and preparing yourself to begin working with a Core Beastie. That's fantastic.

The amazing and very special thing about Core Beasties is that when you discover one and get to know it, it's like coming home to yourself. This is the good stuff.

When we connect with the energy of an animal or, for that matter, anything in nature – a tree, a rock – we're connecting with its vibration or inherent spirit. We feel that energy when, for example, we see a beautiful oak tree or a wild flower and recognize its beauty. Are you with me? It's kind of like being in the company of a person who's very positive, in tune with you, and uplifting. You become uplifted by being with them.

All things in nature have an inherently high vibration. If that sounds weird or if you find yourself arguing with it, just pretend it's true while you're reading this paragraph. Compared to humans, wild Beasties don't resist their own existence. They're in a wonderful state of energetic flow. As humans, if we can get into that state, we can begin to powerfully manifest a life we love.

What I absolutely adore about this work is that it gets me out of my head and into my heart, really connecting me with my intuitive or divine self, which has a deep, vast knowledge and knows exactly how to go about making things happen. This shift toward the heart also brings greater peace. As I've worked with Beasties, I've discovered a sense of real peace and joy that I hadn't found before. I'd love to help you find that, too.

A Core Beastie that's with you over a lifetime plays an empowering and protective role. The practice of shamanism, used around the globe for tens of thousands of years, includes connecting with Core Beasties. Shamanism views illness or mental crisis as a result of a Core Beastie having left or abandoned that person. If a person is ill, a shaman might look to see if the problem has to do with their relationship with their Core Beastie.

Why would a Core Beastie abandon someone? It may happen if we don't honor it or pay attention to its messages. Beasties

YOU ARE UPLIFTED BY BEING WITH CORE BEASTIES!

come to us and have free will to leave if they choose. A relationship with a Core Beastie is a two-way street. When we honor the relationship, we help to maintain its strength and the benefits of that great connection.

Core Beasties are some of the most amazing, wonderful teachers, healers, and protectors I've ever met. Oddly enough, I've found that most of us are more willing to accept guidance from a Core Beastie than from our spouses, parents, or other "helpful" people in our lives (giggle).

I'm excited for you to discover your first Core Beastie so you can get to work with it. There are different ways of discovering a Core Beastie. Before we look at them, let's cover a few other concepts and issues.

Core Beasties Gone Wild

Core Beasties tend to be wild, as a general rule. A wild Beastie lives in surrender to its own self and is able to fully express its heart's desires without limits. It has an inherently high vibration. Domestic animals, on the other hand – such as dogs, cats, and domesticated horses – often have a vibration impacted by humans. In a sense, a domesticated animal is in service to humans.

COULD
MY DOG
BE MY
CORE
BEASTIE
?

People ask me, "Could my dog be my Core Beastie?" A dog might be a portal to discovering a Core Beastie – that often happens. Pets, it seems to me, are on a somewhat higher vibration and have much to teach us about living tuned in to our own hearts. My own dogs, Buttercup and Spirit, have wonderful vibrations to connect with. If your connection with your dog is where you feel most comfortable right now, I'd definitely work with that relationship. I suggest you begin there, if that's what feels exciting to you. As often happens, it may lead you to opening up to a wild Beastie later.

Keep in mind that Core Beasties can be mythical or prehistoric creatures, like dragons, unicorns, or dinosaurs – so be open to them as well. The principles are the same.

Hello, Beastie!

Your Core Beastie will choose you. Now, I don't mean it will walk (or swim or fly) up to you and tap you on the shoulder. Then again, it just might! It will show itself to you many times, so be aware of what's showing up for you and try not to resist it. Don't worry if you find that you're trying to force it. You may have some resistance, but your true Core Beastie *will* continue to show up. Once you do connect with it, it'll really feel wonderful, like connecting with a deep personal truth about yourself that's somehow been forgotten or diminished.

The Beastie that chooses you does so because it has perfect, unique messages, strengths, and teachings for you. You may want your Core Beastie to be a soaring eagle because your ego wants it to be an eagle, even though another Beastie is trying to get your attention, so be aware that your ego could get in the way of finding a Core Beastie. If it does, you'll find the process of connecting with your Core Beastie more difficult and challenging. I know I did.

Is There a Zoo in You?

Most traditions believe that people have one Core Beastie, but several believe you can work with up to a hundred. It's important to realize that to actually work with a hundred Core Beasties would require quite a bit of energy and time on your side to properly maintain those relationships and keep them in order.

To begin with, I invite you to explore a single Core Beastie. This is a situation where more is not necessarily better. What's important is the quality of the relationship.

Let's Begin

Let yourself be drawn to the power of any Beasties you love. Notice what Beasties you admire and are really interested in. Does one pop into your head instantly? Then you're probably on the right track. Or are you like me and several Beasties pop into your mind?

I've discovered that, for many people, the discovery of a Core Beastie happens fairly quickly once they learn what to look for. After brief contemplation of the questions below, they often instantly know.

To tune in to who your Core Beastie is, ask yourself questions like these:

❀❀ Did you have a well-loved stuffed animal as a kid?

❀❀ Have you had recurring dreams where a certain animal shows up over and over again?

❀❀ What was the first animal you'd run to at the museum or zoo when you were a child?

❀❀ Have you ever had an incredible encounter with a wild animal? It could be an attack, a very unusual sighting, or an extremely unusual occurrence.

   sarah bamford seidelmann m.d. | www.whatthewalrusknows.com

In ancient indigenous societies, if someone was attacked by a Beastie and survived the attack, it was often thought that that was the person's initiation into becoming a shaman, and they'd probably be working with the medicine, or spirit, of that Beastie. If you've ever been bit by a snake, attacked by a wild animal, or had another kind of extraordinary encounter, that animal may be a Core Beastie for you.

Still stumped? Try being a detective.

Look around your home and notice whether you have artwork, figurines, fabric, objects, jewelry, DVDs, photography, or anything else with the recurring image of a particular animal on it. We can sometimes be surprised that subconsciously we've already collected many images or objects featuring the same animal – without being completely aware of it. I was once on a phone call with someone who wasn't sure at all what his Core Beastie was. Then, all of a sudden, he shouted, "Wait a minute! You're not going to believe what's hanging over my fireplace! Of course I know what my Core Beastie is. It's the fox!" Since childhood, the fox had figured prominently in his life. He'd just forgotten. Those surprise discoveries around the home can be wonderful clues about what your Core Beastie might be.

Not everyone will have a quick, intuitive knowing of what their Core Beastie is. Others are more like me. As I began answering questions and exploring possibilities, I generated quite a long list of Beasties I thought might be my Core Beastie. The process of narrowing it down and identifying my Core Beastie took a while. If this is happening to you, go ahead and generate a list – and stay curious and open.

Hold out your hands to feel the luxury of sunbeams.

Helen Keller

There are a few things you can do to see if a Beastie that appears is your Core Beastie. Try finishing this sentence: "I know the _____ is my Core Beastie because...." For example, "I know the whale is my Core Beastie because I had a stuffed whale as a kid that was absolutely my best friend and because I've always been completely enamored with whales. I've seen them. This feels true and right. This is my Core Beastie." Play around with knowing to see how it feels.

Next, I'd invite you to investigate further to learn more about the Beastie. Learning more about your Core Beastie or a potential Core Beastie is a way to honor it and gain understanding about what it has to offer you. See the Resource Guide in this book for suggestions about where to explore.

If you're like I was and you have many Core Beastie candidates, pick one Beastie today and learn more about it. Your responses to what you learn can help you determine whether it's a Core Beastie for you. What you're looking for is an internal resonance with your own essential self or soul – your own core. If a connection with a particular Core Beastie feels like truth, then you're probably landing on the perfect one for you. Nobody else can tell you what your Core Beastie is just by talking with you, but discussing your ideas with a nonjudgmental and fabulous person, a coach, or a favorite shaman can help.

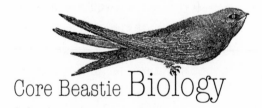

Core Beastie Biology

When exploring to learn about a Core Beastie, the first step is to study its biology and get to know its life cycle. How long does it take to reproduce? Is it a short cycle, like two weeks, as it is for flies? Or is it more like an elephant's two-year gestation period? This may give you insight into how long your own creative projects may take or how long it may take for your new endeavors to manifest.

Is this Beastie mostly diurnal – operating during the day – or is it more of a nocturnal animal? Is it predominately active during dusk and dawn? This may indicate best times for you to work productively. For instance, if you work with the owl as a Core Beastie, your best thinking may occur after dark.

In a marvelous moment of discovery, a dear friend lifted her hair up to reveal that she, like an owl, had one ear positioned lower than the other! This fit with the physical characteristics of the owl. That and all the other signs pointed her in the direction of the owl as a Core Beastie. These are the kinds of magic synchronicities that may show up for you as confirmation.

In what habitat does this Beastie appear? Where does it thrive? Does it thrive in the deep forest? Is it more at home in the open desert? Or in marshland or a jungle or on a mountain? Do you feel drawn to a similar landscape or climate?

What are this Beastie's normal behaviors? When it's being social, how does it communicate? How does it find a mate? How does it mate? How does it parent? Is it solitary, like the eagle, or does it like to hang out in large groups and be gregarious, like the walrus?

What are this Beastie's adaptations? Does it change color to protect itself? Does it bristle its quills? Does it freeze as a defense strategy, like the rabbit? What are all the unique things about this animal that help it survive and thrive in its particular situation and habitat?

What is this Beastie really, really good at? The whale is good at diving deeply. The leopard is extremely patient – while hunting, it will remain perfectly still for very long periods of time, waiting for just the right moment to strike. If you're drawn to the leopard as a Core Beastie, you can ask yourself if there's something you need to be extremely patient with, waiting for the perfect moment so your hunt will be successful – so you'll have a successful outcome to your situation. Leopards and many other large cats are sprinters, built for short bursts of speed rather than the marathon pace of the wolf, who's built to trot at a four to five mile per hour pace almost endlessly. How could your knowledge about a Core Beastie's habits and biology inform your work style? If the whale is your Core Beastie, perhaps it's powerful for you to metaphorically cycle between submerging/diving deep and periodically surfacing?

How does this Beastie eat? Is it vegetarian? Or more of an omnivore, like the bear? Our Core Beastie's eating habits offer clues about how we may want to eat or feed ourselves.

As you learn more about the Beastie, notice what resonates and feels true for you. Those are the bits that may be most powerful for you. For example, if your Core Beastie is a manatee and you're feeling out of sorts or low on energy, you might follow the manatee's habits and switch to a diet that's high in greens. Or it might help to become more manatee-like and simply float or glide through your day. Or you might feel drawn to making contact with water, gliding in the shallows to reconnect with the manatee's peaceful energy. Manatees avoid deep diving and prefer the shallows. This could indicate that going too deep into investigating a topic is not your strength – you may prefer to know just enough. If your Core Beastie is the manatee, the shallows may be your sweet spot.

And we are nature. We are nature seeing nature. The red-winged blackbird flies in us...

Susan Griffin

Some people, after reading about a particular Beastie, have a big **Aha!** It may feel like, **Yes! This is my Core Beastie!** That makes it very simple. Then the only job is to get to know your Beastie and deepen the relationship.

But what if, after all your exploring, you still have a list of candidates, like I did? This can be frustrating for an action-oriented person (like me). Don't despair! Take a deep breath and be patient. This is sacred stuff we're working with and there's no rush. The wait is worth it. I suggest you continue to explore one candidate from your list at a time, learning more about each one in turn and having fun as you go along. Eventually, you'll discover one that feels more powerful and meaningful for you than the others. There are some shortcuts, too. Try my suggestions below and see where they take you.

Core Beastie Dreams

One of the many ways of discovering a Core Beastie is to use your dreams. Right before you go to sleep at night, ask for a dream to show you what your Core Beastie is. We recall and are aware of dreams best when we're well rested, so if you try this, it's good to be able to sleep in and be well rested by the time you wake up. You also might want to keep a notebook beside your bed in case you wake up in the middle of the night and remember a dream. Then you can quickly scribble it down while it's still fresh.

Once, when I was on a trip to Africa, just before going to bed I asked for a sign of a Core Beastie to show up in my dreams. I went on to have a bad dream that night. The next morning at breakfast, I told my friend about the carved, black sign with a black mamba snake that had showed up in my dream. Before that night, we'd been talking about black mamba snakes, which are extremely poisonous. In my dream, when I saw the sign I shouted, "Noooooo ...," and the sign fell away. As I was telling my friend about the dream, I'd actually forgotten I'd asked for a Core Beastie to give me a sign. My friend had to remind me. Talk about resistance!

I resisted that black mamba snake because it felt scary to me. But I went ahead and explored it anyway, knowing that Beasties that frighten us can be powerful to work with. I found out that the snake is a powerful symbol for healers. In my dream, the snake was swirled around a stick, like the Caduceus, the Greek mythological symbol for a healer. Snakes are also masters of transformation and change. As I thought about being a physician and a life coach, and about all the changes I was going through, those connections made sense to me. Months later, a mentor told me that snake, to her, symbolized Kundalini – the potential power we all have within us. Wow! That led me even further down the path of discovery.

So if you discover a Beastie that you know might be powerful, but you're frightened or not too happy about it, please realize that more will be revealed. As you learn more about it, you may find that Beastie being transformed into a powerful ally.

Core Beastie Meditation

Another powerful way to invite a connection with a Core Beastie is to set aside some time, get quiet, and meditate for a bit, asking that a Core Beastie show up for you.

Someone I know who did this started by sitting quietly holding her guitar because she's finds that a relaxing thing to do. As she was meditating, a wolf popped into her consciousness. It felt like a surprise. She thought, *Really, a wolf?* That's often how a Core Beastie's appearance will feel, like it's coming out of left field. But as she read and explored and learned more about the wolf, it began to grow in importance and have a deep resonance for her. She was a professor, and the wolf's essence seemed to fit perfectly with her lifelong love of teaching and mentoring. Her father had been a powerful and (at times) intimidating teacher, yet was incredibly patient with her, so that felt like a magical and empowering connection, too. She came to realize how strong and powerful her own purpose and life were with the wolf as her Core Beastie.

This is what happens when we identify and begin to align with a Core Beastie. We start to recognize the strength offered through the connection, and we see that more and more of its strengths exist within ourselves.

Core Beastie Shamanic Journeys

I was so stuck in my intellect when I began this exploration of Beasties that I didn't have my first successful connection with a Core Beastie until I did a shamanic journey. Shamanic journeying is one of the most amazing, uplifting, and healing practices I've ever encountered. I continue to do it on a regular basis. Sound

...ONE OF THE MOST AMAZING, UPLIFING, AND HEALING PRACTICES I'VE EVER ENCOUNTERED.

strange? Well, read on. It's actually more normal than you may realize, as it's been going on all over the world for tens of thousands of years. Why haven't you heard of this before? Don't worry, it came as a surprise to me, too. It is pretty out there, but, let me tell you, it's too wonderful to be relegated only to the realm of hippies and new-agers. There's currently a wonderful resurgence of people sharing this knowledge.

Shamanism is an ancient practice that's been used all over the world. Many different tribes, from South America to Mongolia and Africa, use drumming or rattling as a way of traveling into an alternate state of consciousness. The fancy anthropological term for drumming or rattling is "sonic driving" (I think the more legit and logical their terms sound, the more research grants they get!). Though this shamanic sonic driving has been around forever, most of us haven't had much contact with it. No worries. You can learn now and catch up.

A shamanic journey is a way to travel to the lower world – not to be confused with the underworld. The lower world is a spiritual place (what the official Foundation for Shamanic Studies calls "non-ordinary reality"), where Core Beastie spirits reside. In shamanism, if someone is ill, the shaman's job may be to travel to that spiritual realm and help them reconnect with their Core Beastie.

What's wonderful and amazing is that you don't have to be a shaman to visit that world. Shamanic journeying is not reserved only for those who've devoted their lives to the craft. Everyone and anyone who's willing to learn the tools can do it.

In indigenous cultures, it was considered a privilege to learn to connect with the natural world – to receive its teachings and learn its magic. Individuals in those cultures had varying degrees of ability to connect with non-ordinary reality. Those with a powerful connection became the lead healers of their group.

The power of shamans is their ability to travel to the spirit realms by entering an altered state of consciousness at will. They do this to perform healings, do psychopomp work (helping confused spirits of the dead to cross over), and accomplish other amazing stuff. It's challenging to correlate what a shaman does to modern allopathic medicine. The shaman could be considered a doctor of the heart and mind. If forced to categorize them, we could call a shaman a cardio-neurosurgeon-psychiatrist. Suffice it to say that the shaman is a holistic practitioner rather than a specialist.

Shamans believe we "see" with our hearts. Even hard science is beginning to find evidence that the heart is in communication with every cell in the body. This new idea radically flies in the face of what we formerly believed – that the brain was the end-all be-all boss of the body. The heart as the co-coordinator of the body is perfectly in balance with the world of the shaman.

Similar methodologies for shamanic journeying are used by different cultures all over the world: We enter an altered state of consciousness via listening to drumbeats or rattling. A specific rhythm takes us into a theta brainwave state – an altered state of consciousness where we're able to enter the lower realm and meet and communicate with a Core Beastie. Typically, we enter the lower world by passing through a small crack in the earth, like through a cave or a tree root or a lake.

If you're interested in playing with this shamanic journey idea on your own, you can start by listening to a drumming CD — there are many available. I really love ones that also have rattles or berimbau (traditional stringed instruments) as, for me, they seem to add to the depth and richness of the journey experience. Be sure the drumming recording you listen to is designed for the purpose of shamanic journeying and has a callback sequence. The callback is important, as it's designed to literally call you back to our ordinary reality. My recommendations for drumming CDs can be found in the Resource Guide section of this book.

When journeying, you must, first and foremost, be focused and full of intention and purpose. Write your intention down and say it out loud a few times. A great intention for a first shamanic journey could be, "I'd like to meet my Core Beastie and get to know it." Remember your intention.

My Shamanic teacher tells me the spirits of the Beasties like scents and flames (that makes a lot of sense to me as my own spirit does, too), so you may also want to light a candle or burn some incense you like, in order to invite the Beastie spirits in.

As you begin, allow your heart to be open. Think of a favorite place out in nature that you love and are very familiar with. Spend a few moments there in your imagination. Next, imagine a place where you could enter the lower world. It could be via a crack in a stone next to the creek, through a body of water, down a tree root, into a tiny rabbit burrow. The size of the way down is not important, as this is spirit travel, after all. Your carcass stays put. Besides being focused and intentional, this imagining is really the only "work" you need to do. Imagination or visualization is simply a way of creating an image of something that does not yet exist in ordinary reality.

As you go down to enter the lower world, notice your surroundings. What's the texture of the cave wall you're following down? Or what's the structure of the stones in the tunnel you're passing through? Focusing on details, like what's sensual and textural, can be vitally helpful to the process.

At the end of the downward journey, notice an exit point, the place that marks your arrival into the lower world. Upon arrival, just open up all your senses to the nature of the place. The lower world is home to jungles, mountains, forests, plains, marshes, beaches, and any number of other lovely natural places. What do you see, sniff, taste, or realize as you look around and experience this place?

Notice whether there are any Beasties there. If you sense a Beastie, simply ask it, "Are you my Core Beastie?" They will answer you, though it may be a telepathic answer. You'll find that you don't have to speak out loud in the lower world but can communicate wordlessly some or all of the time.

A Beastie in the lower world may point you to another Beastie. People often successfully discover a Core Beastie on the first journey. If you do, ask the Beastie what it has to teach you or offer you for strength. Thank it for showing up and for any and all gifts it offers you.

The Beasties of the lower world are compassionate and loving and have our best interests at heart. That means they can be as demanding as your college organic chemistry professor, who also only wanted what's best for you. Worthy adversaries and teachers are there in the lower world, as are nurturing, mothering spirits. Your Core Beastie will be absolutely perfect for you. In the beginning, my Core Beastie showed me a lot of unconditional love – and that was just exactly what I needed.

If you're not comfortable with the idea of entering an altered state of consciousness, no problem. Even though I was fascinated by the idea of shamanism, it took me quite a while to go on my first journey. Surrendering like that seemed frightening. Now I'm so glad I did it because of the wonderful experiences and connections I've found.

Shamanic journeying has been a real surprise and delight in my life. I love shamanic journeying because when we surrender, the truth can be revealed. It may sound so odd, but there's much love there for you if you're willing to investigate it.

You may be more familiar or comfortable with the idea of a visualization, which is a variation on the theme of taking a journey of the imagination. If so, explore visualizing to meet with a Core Beastie. Visualize yourself entering a beautiful, pleasing place in nature and see what Beastie shows up with a message or a teaching for you.

Explore in a way that seems easy and fun and non-intimidating. That will be the best way for you to meet a Core Beastie.

More Core Beastie Discovery Options

Sometimes, the process of discovering a Core Beastie may feel like too much pressure, or you may have difficulty making what feels like a meaningful connection with a Core Beastie. If you've been trying lots of things and nothing seems to be working, you can explore other systems that already exist, like the Native American and Chinese zodiac systems or the symbology of saints

(saints often have animals associated with them). If this way of discovering a Core Beastie sounds fun to you, and if you remain curious, then it will likely lead you down a path of self-discovery.

Using a reference guide for one of the zodiac systems, you can use your birth year and date to see what Beastie is associated with your specific birth date. Or, using a resource about saints, you can browse and explore, starting with associations you're drawn to. For instance, you can look up your own name and see if there's a saint associated with that name and, if so, what Beastie might be connected with it.

Is This Core Beastie for Me?

People often ask, "How do I know if this Core Beastie is the right one for me?" First of all, working with the powerful energies of Core Beasties is not something that needs to be rushed. Be patient. Your Core Beastie will keep showing up, and your connection will eventually become clear. When you know, you'll know.

Knowing doesn't need to shift your world on its axis. It can feel soft as a feather. Knowing feels *right*, however that feels to you. It will taste of truth. Only you know what that tastes like for you.

"Bad" or Ferocious Core Beasties

People also ask, "What if a certain Beastie keeps showing up, but I don't like that Beastie?" In that case, sometimes what's needed is to learn more.

Please remember that in the great web of life each Beastie is perfectly designed to serve its unique purpose – just as you're designed to do. Often, it's what we don't understand that we fear or dismiss.

Here's an example of how understanding can help connect us with a Core Beastie ...

A woman called in to our *Squirrel! Radio* show one day to tell us that bears kept showing up for her, but she didn't want the bear as her Core Beastie because she didn't like them. We asked her to tell us more about why she didn't like them.

She said she'd seen a movie where a grizzly bear stalked people and that seemed negative to her. She'd also seen a nature film where a mother bear decided it was time for her cubs to become independent, so she chased them up a tree and ran off. When the cubs kept climbing down the tree, the mother bear went again to growl at them ferociously and chase them back up. The caller thought that seemed overly cruel. How could a mother do that to her children?

Tami McCall, *Squirrel! Radio* co-founder and a fellow coach, asked the caller if she had children. She did. Her kids were about 12 and 13. Tami intuitively offered the idea that maybe the caller was uncomfortable with that image of a mother bear because her own children weren't yet ready to be independent.

Bears are extremely solitary. Once they're grown, they typically don't hunt together or depend on each other, so being independent is a crucial set of skills the mother bear teaches her children. The power of the mother bear is that she raises cubs to become independent and to fend for themselves. And she knows when they're ready to be on their own. As we talked, the caller breathed a huge sigh of relief because that idea really resonated with her. She realized that she, too, would know when the right time came to encourage her children to be more independent.

As the caller began to open up to the idea of bear as her Core Beastie, she started remembering positive experiences about bears, like when she and her brothers, as kids, used to watch a show that featured a bear. They'd dress up their dog, pretending he was a bear. She remembered feeling a wonderful, joyful presence whenever they did that. It often happens that as we discover a Core Beastie and begin to accept it, we see all the ways it has shown up in our past.

Sometimes, what we need to know about our Core Beastie is right under our noses, once we begin to think about it. Bear is a Core Beastie for me, too, as I discovered through a shamanic journey. Afterwards, I looked back over my life and saw that I'd had many powerful dreams with bears in them. Also, when I was a kid camping in Canada with my dad, we saw what we thought was a bear in the coals of our campfire one night. We called it the spirit of the bear. About a month before I discovered that bear is a Core Beastie for me, I had an extraordinary sighting of a mother bear and three cubs.

Symbolism and meanings shift for each person examining a connection with a Core Beastie, even if they have the same Core Beastie. That day on *Squirrel! Radio*, I also had a huge *Aha!*, though it was different from our caller's. I began to understand my own fierce need for my own children to be independent. Even though the caller and I were looking at the same Beastie – the bear – we each saw a unique meaning.

SOMETIMES... WHAT WE NEED TO KNOW ABOUT OUR CORE BEASTIE IS RIGHT UNDER OUR NOSES...

Something to keep in mind is that it can be powerful to know the Core Beastie for a sibling, child, or loved one you want to connect with more deeply. The understanding you gain about them can be priceless and powerful.

Your Core Beastie really will keep showing up and giving you options for noticing it. You'll have plenty of chances to connect. Like with all things divine, there's no rush. Simply explore, be open, be patient, and allow.

I wish you the fun of discovering your Core Beastie and connecting easily with them. Once you do, you can deepen your relationship to find greater and greater strength, joy, and power. That's what the next chapter is all about.

CORE BEASTIES
– DIVING DEEPER –

"Divination is not a rival form of knowledge;
it is a part of the main body
of knowledge itself."

Michel Foucault

Core Beasties – Diving Deeper

When you deepen your relationship with a Core Beastie, you can create what you want in your life with less effort. Whether you want an intimate relationship, more abundance, or anything else, your partnership with a Core Beastie can be a gateway to making it happen magically.

A relationship with a Core Beastie is like having a mentor who encourages you and really sees what's possible for you. It's a two-way street: You get out of it what you put in. Like with any relationship – with an amazing friend, a lover, or a human mentor – when we honor a relationship with a Core Beastie, it thrives. So do we.

How do we deepen a Core Beastie relationship? First, it's important to learn as much as possible about your Core Beastie, through whatever resources appeal to you. The more you know about your Core Beastie, the deeper the relationship will be, so that's the most basic thing to do initially. You'll find suggestions for getting to know your Core Beastie in the previous chapter. Once you know a lot about your Core Beastie, even if you're still continuing to learn more, you can also do other things to deepen the relationship.

Forging a wonderful, strong relationship with a Core Beastie is like cracking open a doorway into a vast world of nature and other Beasties. By entering, you open yourself to receiving many more messages and making further discoveries. Are you willing to devote a bit of time and research on this? There's a big payoff.

Get to Know Your Beastie Over Coffee

After you've learned about your Core Beastie, the next thing I suggest is having a conversation with it. It might sound like a strange thing to do, but I've found it can be a powerful and simple way to connect.

Connecting with your Core Beastie is like having a conversation with your divine self, or what some people call the "sacred self." Your divine self contrasts with your social self. The social self is externally motivated. It follows the rules, takes tests, and does things to make sure people like you. A good, strong social self is critical for being able to thrive in community. Without it, we wouldn't be able to share our life's purpose effectively or function in society. And yet, if we listen to our social self to the exclusion of our divine or sacred self, we miss out on a lot of the magic in life.

The divine self knows how powerful we are. The divine self is connected to the universe – or the Earth, or God, depending on your views. The divine self is a fearless part of us that's completely at peace with who we are and knows we are powerful beyond measure. That's a pretty wonderful kind of self to connect with when we're trying to manifest big and fabulous things in our lives.

So how do you have a divine and sacred conversation with your Core Beastie? I invite you to set aside some quiet time when you're not going to be disturbed. Close the door, turn off the phone, and sit quietly. You could drink coffee or tea and offer your Core Beastie something, too. Beastie energies enjoy scents – like incense, candles, or whatever else that comes to mind that you think they might enjoy.

If it helps, close your eyes. Think of your Core Beastie and ask it a question. The question you ask could be anything. It might be about what strength it has that it could offer you right now. Or how it would advise you to proceed in a particular situation. Or you may simply want to ask it to tell you more about itself. You could ask it what it would like you to know about it. This is a friendship, so it's appropriate to be polite and ask things like, "What would you like to tell me about yourself?" After asking a question, presume you're going to get a reply. This is key. Act as though you *know* you'll get an answer. Send out that intention.

More About Asking Questions

You can access the wisdom of your Core Beastie anytime you like by asking questions. Excellent types of questions to ask your Beastie begin with the open-ended question words interviewers and reporters use:

WHO   (... shall I ask to help me with my project at work?)

WHAT   (... is this recent kidney problem here to teach me?)

WHERE   (... can I find nirvana?)

WHY   (... can't I remember people's names at a networking function?)

HOW   (... do I recover the intense original feelings of passion in relationship now that we've been married for five years? ... will I know when it's a good time to make the move to Dubai?)

sarah bamford seidelmann m.d. | www.whatthewalrusknows.com

It's best to avoid asking yes or no questions or asking for specific times or dates, as (of course) there's no concept of time in the divine field or the spirit world. For that reason, any time-specific answer you receive is likely to be inaccurate.

I've found that my Core Beastie's responses to my questions are often very simple answers of very few words. For me, their responses are communicated telepathically. You may receive your answers differently – through a sensation, a scent, a sound, or some other way.

Here's an example of asking a Core Beastie a question. This past summer we were having an extremely challenging time getting one of our kids to go to bed at night. She kept getting up and coming out of her room. The challenge had reached a fever pitch and we were at wit's end figuring out how to deal with it. I went out to a marsh and sat for a while in a place I knew a local bear had been to and asked my bear Core Beastie, "What do I need to know to make this work so we can have peace and so she can feel good, too?" The response I got back was, "Hug her." It came to me as a knowing from within, and it felt very true and right.

As I sat and thought about this answer, I realized it would probably be a good idea to reverse the order of our bedtime ritual of reading stories, and then hugging at the end. Since she'd been acting up so much lately, sometimes the hugs got left out by the time all the other things had been dealt with. Kids need to know they're loved, no matter what. Switching and hugging first worked, and bedtimes became more peaceful.

From what people have told me about their conversations with Core Beasties, the answers they receive also tend to be brief. And usually there will be no sense of urgency in the answer. As my fellow coach Indrani Goradia loves to say, "With the sacred, there is no hurry."

When you get a response to your question, if it's coming from your Core Beastie, it will feel like truth. It will feel peaceful and soft, like a feather. If it feels harsh or heavy-handed, it may be your ego or your left brain trying to muscle in and say something self-serving. If that happens, sit quietly and ask the question again. Or it could be that your Beastie wants you to take some action that you're resisting. In either of those cases, you may want to set that Q and A session aside for a bit and return to it after some time has passed. It's fine if you're doubting that this process is even working. Just try setting the doubt aside and see what happens – see if the response you seemed to get is helpful when you apply it to your life.

It's fun to play with the concept of asking questions. It's a way of calling your Core Beastie to your side. You can do it anytime and anywhere. If you have a good relationship with your Core Beastie, it will be there for you when you ask.

Shamanic Journeys

Using shamanic journeying as a way to connect with the lower world and get more information about potential Core Beasties was introduced in the previous chapter. Once you've identified your Core Beastie, you can take shamanic journeys to visit with it. While there, you can ask questions, ask for a healing, find out more about what its world is all about, or simply play.

I've found shamanic journeying to be one of the most delightful, powerful, wacky, wild, and fabulous ways to learn, gain insight, receive healing, and connect. The lower world is populated with compassionate and loving spirits that want to help you.

If a shamanic journey sounds fun to you, try it out. If it sounds scary or intimidating or strange, then it may not be for you. That's okay. Keep reading. There are more options to come. Notice what feels good to you to try, and try it.

Stories and Mythology

Reading about your Core Beastie's mythology may offer insights into your life and what your Core Beastie is here to show and teach you. I invite you to deepen your relationship by exploring the stories associated with it over time. Some stories may be ancient. There are many Beasties associated with Greek mythology and Hindu deities. For example, the Hindu god Ganesha – remover of obstacles and lord of all new beginnings – is depicted with the head of an elephant.

Google your Core Beastie along with the word "mythology" or "legend" and see what pops up. My hunch is that this exploration will lead to many divine synchronicities and that even more will be revealed to you about the power of your Core Beastie for you. As always, simply notice what piques your interest and ignore the rest. If there's something you're meant to focus on, it'll keep showing up.

One of the Core Beasties I work with is bear. Many native tribes on the Northwest Coast of North America tell a similar story about a young woman who became lost in the woods and was befriended by a bear. At first, she was afraid of the bear, but the bear was kindly and taught her the ways of the forest, thus saving her life. In the tale, she eventually becomes the bear's wife, growing thick hair and hunting like a bear. When the couple have children, at first she tries to teach them the ways of both bears and humans, but her human family won't accept her marriage to the bear. Her human family ends up killing her bear husband. At that point, she decides to break completely with the ways of humans and become fully a bear.

A story like this can bring up interesting ways of exploring the wisdom of a Core Beastie. This story could be speaking about being lost but finding refuge and learning something new from someone. Or about needing to step away from family and find one's own way of living in the world, to become more fully oneself. Or there may be other connections with the story, depending on who's interpreting it. When you delve into a story about your Core Beastie, be open to whatever insights and connections pop up for you.

I knew someone who thought the vulture might be his Core Beastie, but he was having trouble accepting it, feeling that the vulture wasn't very attractive or likeable. Then he discovered a story from South America about the vulture. In the story, the Earth and Sun had moved too close to each other and the powerful energy and heat of the sun began to scorch the Earth, causing a lot of problems. The animals got together and said, "We've got to get the Sun further away from the Earth, otherwise the Earth is going to be destroyed." Many animals did their best to move the Sun further away, but none of them were successful. Finally, the vulture, the most beautiful and powerful bird, decided to take it upon himself to do the job. He flew to the Sun and moved it away from the Earth, but in the process scorched his head feathers and lost his beauty. Through this tale, the vulture can be seen as a wonderful hero who had the guts to do something dangerous, risking his vanity and beauty to save Earth and all its creatures.

Another example of a Beastie people often have resistance to – I know I did – is the snake. In many ways, this makes sense, as reptiles are a bit harder for us to relate to than mammals, which are more similar to us in their essential biology. Australian Aboriginals tell about the rainbow serpent, the powerful creator who birthed the universe. In the Aboriginal world, she's the mother of all creation. As she slithered through the earth, she created the rivers and lakes. In their story, the snake is a mother and a powerful manifestor. I've encountered snakes in shamanic journeys that were fierce instructors, asking a lot of me. On more than one shamanic journey, I've met a snake with a sense of humor that was pretty laid back and a bit bored. Doesn't that sound strange and fun? That's what's so magical about shamanic journeying. Through it, I've become comfortable with snakes. I've lost my fear. In part, this is what connections with Beasties can do for us. They heal us and prepare us to get out into the world and do the work we were put here to do … courageously.

There are many cultures with stories about Beasties and many resources for discovering them. Look around and find out what your Core Beastie's been up to over the millennia and see what resonates with you.

Create a Beastie Altar   OBJECTS CARRY POWER & ENERGY TOO...

Like everything in the world, objects carry power and energy. This is one of the main tenets of the shamanic way of life. A way to connect with your Core Beastie on a daily basis in a visual way is to create a little altar to honor its energies and unique gifts to you. This can be done very simply, by clearing a bit of space on a shelf or dresser and collecting things there that that appeal to you and have to do with your Core Beastie. There doesn't have to be much – even one picture you see every day can give you a greater feeling of connection.

I want to make the point that this altar is not about worshipping your Core Beastie, as that would imply that it has more potential power than you. We're all powerful – no one of us more than any other. A Core Beastie altar is about honoring it – appreciating it and its strength and beauty.

When you're gathering things for a Core Beastie altar, the possibilities are endless: a photograph of the Beastie, a symbol that represents it, a feather, a piece of artwork, a cloth, a sculpture or figurine. You could also light a candle that in some way – by its color or scent or in other ways – reminds you of your Core Beastie.

Several years ago, my daughter gave me a little bear created out of clay and fired with a shiny, black glaze. I keep it on my desk to honor my Core Beastie and remind me of bear's strengths, which are mine, too. It helps me feel empowered and strong and reminds me to honor the power of the bear.

How can you have fun playing with the altar idea? What appeals to you as a way to honor your Core Beastie? Take some time to discover an object that speaks to you about your Core Beastie and feels powerful and delightful and wonderful.

I know several people who wear jewelry that reminds them of their Core Beastie. One friend has a bracelet with a feather that reminds her of her eagle Core Beastie. I once met a man, an entrepreneur, whose Core Beastie is a hummingbird. He wears a hummingbird necklace every day. When I met him, I thought his hummingbird spirit was so obvious – he goes around all day joyfully pollinating all his wonderful entrepreneurial projects. Someone else I know has tattoos of her powerful Core Beasties all over her body – the images are literally a part of her. With their jewelry and tattoos, these people carry their Core Beastie altars around with them.

Some ways of visually connecting with your Core Beastie on a daily basis will appeal to you more than others. Do some experimenting to see what you like. Keep your eyes open for possibilities.

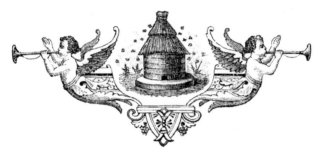

Get Your Creative Mojo Flowing – Play!

Creating imagery is another fun way to explore deepening your relationship with your Core Beastie. Try not to let limiting beliefs about yourself as an artist keep you from exploring this option. I believe we're all artists, even if we've been told we're not.

Any medium works for this exploration, from collage to painting to photography. In the art you create, you can play around with what aspects or characteristics of your Core Beastie you want to connect with. What is its particular form of power? Or way of getting things done? How can you depict that in your art? What imagery feels most powerful?

This doesn't even have to be about creating a finished work of art. Keep it simple. Grab some colored pencils and a tablet at the drugstore. Play. Be willing to do it just for fun. You can use the process to explore your connection with your Core Beastie. If it feels good, put your creation in a spot where you can connect with it often – on a closet door, in the medicine cabinet, on the shelf above the fireplace.

Whether it's through decoupage, oil painting, needlepoint, or using an iPhone application to alter an image, playfully connecting with your Core Beastie through your creative right brain is a powerful way to foster your relationship.

Beastie Vision Boards

A simple way to get into a creative space is to gather, arrange, and paste magazine pictures to make a vision board. Vision boards are used as reminders of what's desired. They're often created through a collage process of gathering images from magazines (or wherever) and pasting them onto a backing, like poster board or cardboard. The images can be arranged any way you like. One vision board I created has a place in the middle for a picture of me, with images of Beasties all around. It can be helpful to keep the vision board in a prominent place where you'll see it every day and be reminded of the Core Beastie energy you want to connect with. You can create a digital vision board if you want, using an online site where you can virtually pin images you like onto a viewing area.

You don't need to only use pictures of your Core Beastie when creating a vision board. You can also gather imagery that speaks to you about the qualities you admire in your Core Beastie, arranging the images in a way that appeals to you. Think about what you admire about your Core Beastie – perhaps their courage, patience, strength, or sensuality. What images depict the particular wisdom, abilities, sensibilities, and energy of your Core Beastie? You can build a vision board like this over time, too, as you find images that fit.

Whether it's by making a vision board or looking through your camera or any other way, how can you use art and creativity to align more with the qualities you admire in your Core Beastie? For example, if the ant is your Core Beastie, you may admire its ability to accomplish big projects by moving one bit of earth at a time. Ants take many tiny steps daily to patiently build giant empires. How could you depict that in a piece of art?

Whatever you admire in your Core Beastie, you possess in yourself. *When you create art to honor your Core Beastie, you also honor yourself.*

To Honor is to Love

A traditional Native American way of showing honor is to leave a bit of cornmeal or tobacco at the base of a tree to thank a totem Beastie for its assistance. In a similar way, you might want to perform a ceremony of some kind to honor your Core Beastie. It could be a private thing or something not so private, depending on what appeals to you.

There's a wonderful story in Brad Steiger's book *Totems* about a woman with snake as her Core Beastie. Every spring when the weather warms up, she'd invite her friends who also had snake as their Core Beastie to a snake party. They'd bake a snake cake and dance and sing and give thanks for the powerful energies of the snake in their lives.

JUMP IN! Ways to play with honoring your Beastie are infinite. Jump in and discover what feels fun to you.

Shapeshifting

Let's put on our anthropologist bush helmets for a moment and delve deeper into some of the ancient ways of deepening a connection with a Core Beastie. If we want to study these other ways of connecting, it helps to act as though we have the beliefs of the indigenous peoples who practiced shamanism.

If you've not previously been exposed to these ideas about shapeshifting, it might seem fairly fantastic or out there to you. Yet I don't want you to miss out on this. It's one of the most powerful techniques I know for exploring a connection with a Core Beastie.

Shapeshifting is the ability to transform into another animal or person or object. In shamanism, it's believed that one can literally become or merge with the spirit of a Beastie. When Native Americans merged with the spirit of a buffalo, for example, they were considered to be merged with all the spirits of all buffalos that ever existed – essentially, with the archetypal buffalo spirit.

In ancient times as well as in the present day, hunters sometimes use shapeshifting. A hunter who shapeshifts into a tree becomes energetically invisible to the animal he's hunting. Hunters in the

Lakota Sioux tribes often shapeshifted into a buffalo the evening before they went out to hunt buffalo, in order to honor the spirit of the animal for (hopefully) providing their family with food, clothing, and fuel. Shapeshifting acknowledged the buffalo's sacrifice for the hunter and his family. Shapeshifting could also provide insight to the hunter about how or where their hunting might be most successful. It was believed that the spirits they merged with were benevolent and had a desire to assist them – just like your Core Beastie does.

In her book *Shapeshifting into Higher Consciousness: How to Heal and Transform Yourself and Our World*, Llyn Roberts writes that because "traditional peoples know that everything is interconnected and that all is infused with energy and power from the same source: a hunter in the Amazon can merge with the qualities of a jaguar to embody the stealth, swiftness and cunning desired to catch his prey; a healer in the high Andes can embody the traits of an active volcano, shapeshifting into the essence of the sacred mountains of his region and engulfing clients in fire balls to incinerate the root of illness; a Bugi navigator in Indonesia can blend with the consciousness of a frigate bird taking imaginary flights across vast ocean expanses to chart his ship's course ...."

By shapeshifting into the Beastie we're working with – becoming one with it, we gain insight and power. You can play with shapeshifting into your Core Beastie by setting aside some time to be alone, getting quiet, declaring your intention, and seeing what happens. Through shapeshifting, you can do what the Beastie does and get sense of them from inside.

From a shamanic perspective, shapeshifting begins with intent. You can state your intent – "I'd like to shapeshift into _____," or "I'd like to become _____," naming the

Beastie – then visualize yourself becoming that Beastie. This process alone can often create an exchange of energy or a shapeshifting transformation.

Though you can explore shapeshifting as a simple visualization, it can be extremely powerful to physically move your body during shapeshifting. For example, you could play a recording of drumming or other pleasing rhythms and dance your Core Beastie. To feel what it's like to move as a Core Beastie is to experience its power on a different, more physical plane. Something happens when, for instance, we say, "I'm going to become the bear," and we begin physically moving like the bear, lumbering around. Then, vibrationally, we're not only mentally lining up with the bear, we're also lining up kinesthetically.

If you're not familiar with how your Core Beastie moves, you may want to spend some time studying its movements. Especially if your Core Beastie is one you wouldn't normally encounter directly, watching it on video can be useful.

If you try shapeshifting as your Core Beastie, I invite you to take some notes after the experience about what it felt like and what occurred to you as you did it. Did you have a new insight? Did you feel more like your Core Beastie? Did you feel stronger or more patient? Were you able to draw on more of the power and unique characteristics of your Core Beastie? What happened?

Shapeshifting and moving around as your Core Beastie is a way of dancing, and dancing is a powerful way of healing ourselves.

If someone ill is presented to a shaman, the shaman will ask three questions:

When did you stop talking and telling stories?

When did you stop singing?

When did you stop dancing?

Those three things – telling stories, singing, and dancing – are integral to our health, wellness, and well-being. When you dance and shapeshift into your Core Beastie, you open the door to a powerful and empowering experience.

Belief Systems

You can also explore your connection with your Core Beastie through other spiritual or belief systems you work with.

If you're a Christian, for example, you might find connections with your Core Beastie through one of the saints associated with your Core Beastie, or by connecting with St. Francis, known for his deep connection with animals and nature.

If you do yoga as part of your spiritual practice, you could include your Core Beastie exploration in a variety of ways. You could pick a Beastie to represent each chakra – either the Beasties traditionally associated with the chakras or any Beastie that appeals to you. The base chakra is traditionally associated with the elephant, which is associated with the Hindu deity Ganesha, lord of new beginnings and remover of all obstacles. The base chakra is the place from which we manifest things in this world. If you're working on manifesting – money, a house, or whatever – you may want to connect with the elephant in your chakra work (even if your Core Beastie isn't the elephant).

If you enjoy working with numerology, you can check out Brad Steiger's book Totems, which includes information about using your Lifepath number and calculating the Soul Urge number of your Beastie. As an example, my Lifepath number is three, which is all about self-expression and communicating who I am – that's my big strength. The Soul Urge number of my bear Core Beastie is seven, which is about having the strength to seek out the mysteries of the universe. I find that exploring this gives me particular strength and wisdom.

By exploring and mining your belief systems in general to see what other layers you can discover, you may find that your relationship with your Core Beastie is deepened and expanded.

Dream Analysis

By analyzing our dreams, even in a basic way, we can deepen our connection with a Core Beastie. A Beastie in a dream is thought to be equivalent to that Beastie showing up in waking life. A Beastie that shows up in a dream once can be a Guest Beastie, bringing you a message. If you have recurring dreams or a big, important dream about a Beastie – one that feels very vivid and powerful – that Beastie is likely to be a Core Beastie for you. If you know your Core Beastie, you can ask it to show up in your dreams, to heal you or give you guidance.

The process is simple. You might find it works better if you're well-rested. Set an intention, either in your mind or written out on a slip of paper. You can say something like, "Tonight I'll get an important message from my Core Beastie," or "A Core Beastie will reveal itself tonight in my dreams." You might want to add to your intention that you remember the dream in detail and can write it down easily when you wake up. You could tuck your written intention under your pillow. Intention can make all the difference, so give it some thought.

Before you go to sleep, put a notebook and pen beside the bed so you can scribble some details as soon as you wake up without having to get up, as that would likely take you away from the sense of the dream. If you get into feeling anxious (*Uh-oh, I'm not remembering anything!*), this process can be more challenging, so after you wake up, as you're recalling the dream, try to stay in that mellow, relaxed, barely awake state. By analyzing the dream – using your notes to help you remember it – you can access very powerful information.

The ancient indigenous cultures knew about the power of dreams. Some of those cultures have created and used what they call "dream-catchers." A dream-catcher is a hoop with webbing inside, but with a hole at the center. It was thought that all the good dreams would pass through the hole and the unhelpful bad dreams would be caught in the webbing. The good dreams that passed through were thought to offer insights about one's destiny and path. Some cultures had a practice of dreaming together as a group to bring about and amplify something the entire community desired. Paying attention to dreams was thought to be important work, as dreams provide vital information, teachings, and clues about how we can be successful, avoid danger, and make our way along the road ahead. I know from my own experience of

A CORE BEASTIE WILL REVEAL ITSELF TONIGHT IN MY DREAMS...

MMMM!

serving on a foundation board that when we join our energies to visualize and dream something wonderful as a community, power is amplified.

It's sometimes surprising, but even scary dreams can have wonderful messages for us. It's been my experience that most nightmares are dreams we didn't complete because we'd exited too soon to get to the positive message. I discovered this by re-entering a few of my own so-called bad dreams, using the techniques of shamanic dreaming. You can learn to do this, too. If you do, I recommend that you develop a secure, solid relationship with a Core Beastie first, so it can accompany you on such a courageous adventure. Perhaps nightmares – waking up before we finish with a dream – are a way of protecting us. When we're ready to take in the message of the whole dream, we'll find it.

A classic and simple way of analyzing dreams is to write down all the symbols that occur in a dream to see if you find a message or an insight there. This method, introduced by Sigmund Freud, presumes that the symbols in a dream represent known or hidden parts of ourselves. Freud postulated that all dreams and their messages are created by the dreamer alone. In shamanism, there's an additional caveat or belief that other energies or spirits (not our own) can intrude on our dreams. Though addressing intrusive spirits in our dreams is beyond the scope of this book, if someone is having debilitating, recurrent nightmares that are causing them to feel dis-spirited, seeking out a shamanic practitioner for assistance may be warranted.

Old dreams, if they feel significant, can still yield helpful information in the present. Whether it's a long-ago old dream or a more recent one, if the dream is long and complicated, it might be easiest to start with decoding only the fragment of the dream with the Beastie in it. It's helpful to use the fragment that felt most significant during the dream, but any fragment will do, really.

Beastie Dream Decoder

Below are examples of a simple method for discovering the messages contained within a dream. You can try it out with a Beastie dream you've had in the past or ask for a new dream about your Core Beastie and decode that one.

Doing this process requires that you become quiet and still so you can hear the replies. Act as if you're going to receive replies to the questions you ask.

THE DREAM
Several years ago, I dreamed that some scary, extremely large, powerful bears were throwing things around in our backyard and acting in ways that were threatening.

THE PROCESS

Interview the Dream Beastie.
Ask what's going on. Ask why it's doing what it's doing and what it's trying to communicate to you.

My question to the Beasties:
Why are you acting so scary and enraged and threatening?
Why are you throwing giant barrels around and growling?

Their Answer:
We're hungry & starving & ticked off! We want you to feed us!

{ *Ask the Beastie what part of*
your life it represents in this dream. }

My question to the Beasties:
What part of my life do you represent?

Their Answer:
We represent your creativity.

{ *Ask the Beastie for its recommendations, advice,*
or insight regarding the part of your life it represents. }

My question to the Beasties:
So, what needs to happen or not happen next in my waking
life? What are your recommendations? What do you advise?

Their Answer:
You need to FEED your creativity. It's hungry.
You'll calm down and become peaceful once your
creativity is fed regularly.

What I took from decoding that dream is that if I feed my
creativity (those bears), I won't be angry and frustrated. I could
also say that to honor my bear as a Core Beastie, I must feed
my creativity. That dream came as I was about to embark on a
sabbatical and as I was beginning, in earnest, to deepen my
commitment to learning to be a coach and exploring what I'm
supposed to do with my life. Dreams often come during times
of big transitions and upheaval, as a way of throwing us a bone.
When we decode the messages of dreams, we can get help
about how proceed. Here's another example of using this
method for dream decoding:

THE DREAM
I was in a boat, holding my fingers out over the edge near the engine. Several humpback whales were gently nudging my fingers. There were a few other passengers on the boat, but the whales weren't coming to any of them, only to me. The boat felt safe to be riding in, but it was moving too fast and was extremely low in the water.

Interview the Dream Beastie.

My question to the Beasties:
Whales, why are you nuzzling me and nibbling at my fingers? Why do you come only to me and not to the others in this boat?

Their Answer:
We like you! We want to connect with you.

{ *Ask the Beastie what part of your life it represents in this dream.* }

My question to the Beasties:
What part of my life do you represent?

Their Answer:
We represent your connection to nature and to the Beasties and, in a larger way, to your professional work as a change agent and coach.

{ *Ask the Beastie for its recommendations, advice, or insight regarding the part of your life it represents.* }

My question to the Beasties:
So, Beasties, what needs to happen or not happen
next in my waking life? What do you advise?
What are your recommendations?

Their Answer:
We advise you to slow down or we won't be able to have this
special interaction. Also, you need to get more buoyant.

That all made perfect sense to me. If I tried to hurry the process
of connecting to nature and to my true calling, I might lose the
magical connection I'd been experiencing. I intuitively knew I
needed to be more light and playful (buoyant) in my work and
shed some ballast in my life – to literally get the lead out so I
could float at a higher level. My ballast included having too
many different projects going on, too many commitments, and
too few boundaries regarding my work.

I invite you to give analyzing your dreams a try, in whatever way
appeals to you. You might like it as an additional option for
connecting on a deeper level with your Core Beastie.

There are so many amazing and fun ways to play with deepening
your relationship with a Core Beastie. Just select one idea that
appeals deeply to you or makes your heart leap with "YES!" That
will be the perfect way to begin. I'm so thrilled for you to enter
into a deeper bond with your Core Beastie because it can change
your life. It's changed mine in the very best of ways.

In the next chapter, I'll show you a few exercises,

including one I call "forest bathing."

TOOLS & EXERCISES

"When we learn to say a deep passionate yes to the things that really matter....then peace begins to settle onto our lives like golden sunlight sifting to a forest floor."

Thomas Kinkade

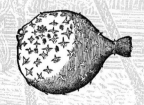

Tools and Exercises

Here are four unique ways to take your Beastie explorations deeper in a more involved way. They can help you discover useful information connected with Beasties that was hidden but can be brought out in the open to assist you.

Daily Beastie Affirmation

Because each Beastie has unique attributes, significant insights may be discovered though focusing on one Beastie every day.

As part of your own daily practice, you can read a different Beastie Manifesto every day.

There are ten items for each Beastie in the Manifestos section. Another option for a daily practice using the Beastie Manifestos is to spice things up by picking a number from one to ten, then reading (for example) the third item in several Manifestos. That would give you a cross-section of Beastie characteristics and insights.

Explore to see what magic might be uncovered by tapping into Beastie brilliance in this way.

UNCOVER MAGIC!

Beastie Revelation

This tool is one I designed to help with accessing the sub-conscious, the part of the mind that's nonlinear and nonlogical, that knows how to connect the dots that create manifestation short-cuts — also called synchronicities.

The Beastie Revelation method is rooted in the ancient practice of divination. The ancients used similar tools or "spiritual technologies," which they relied on to help with healing, discovering the best ways to hunt, and ensuring the survival of the community. The best part is, you don't have to be a shaman living in the Amazon Basin to do this.

To further explain the process, I'll use an example to show how it works.

 Formulate Your Question

It's important that the question be laser-focused and that it begin with one of these words: *how, who, what, why, or where* (not *when*, as time is not a specialty of the subconscious). It should be an open-ended question, to maximize the information to be received. Avoid *yes/no* questions, *should* questions (as in, "Should I buy the house?"), and questions that involve time specifics. Yes/no questions limit the information to be received, because – from a Beastie energy perspective – there is no judgment, no right or wrong implied in the information they give. And because Beastie spirits live outside of time, they aren't concerned with our linear, logical constructs and questions about time.

Here are some examples of well-formulated questions:

 What am I to learn from this diagnosis?

 How can I heal myself regarding (my marriage, my broken friendship, etc.)?

 Who's the best person to mentor me in my career?

EXAMPLE
One day, it seemed that nothing I was trying as a parent was

working, and my frustration was rising. Everyone was up in arms and fighting with each other. I wanted to show my kids that I loved them.

My question: How can I best show my children that I love them?

 Set an Intention
It's important to set an intention to discover useful information from this exercise and receive an answer that's both truthful and helpful.

 Notice and Record the Next Four Beasties
Pay attention to the next four Beasties that catch your attention, the ones that seem to be saying, "Hey, look at me!" – from that fruit fly on the compost heap to the komodo dragon on the television. They may appear outdoors, be seen from the window, or show up in your email in-box. Perhaps they pop up on Facebook, in a magazine, on a billboard, at the side of the road, or in a movie. Write down the Beasties you notice. Depending on what's happening in your day, this could take ten minutes or an entire day.

To expedite the process, you could also flip through the list of Beastie Manifestos at the back of this book (while holding your intention) and record the first four Beasties you see there as you randomly turn the pages.

EXAMPLE
The first four Beasties I came across after clarifying and asking my question, "How can I best show my children that I love them?" were buffalo, leopard, ladybug, and domestic cat.

 Free-Associate
With your list of Beasties in front of you, free-associate the first

word that comes to mind for each animal. No censoring! Even if – especially if – the word that comes to you seems absurd. Remember that this is nonlinear stuff we're accessing in this process, so let go of logic and use the right hemisphere of your brain only, please.

Continue to free-associate, by combining the first two words that came to you and free-associating on them. Those two words combined are a clue to the answer to your question. Muse in a freely associating way on how those clues answer your question.

EXAMPLE

When I did the first round of free associating for my four Beasties, this is what I got:

Buffalo ➡ *Strength*

Leopard ➡ *Sexy*

Ladybug ➡ *Joy*

Domestic Cat ➡ *Common*

In my second round of free associating, this is what I came up with:

Strength + Sexy ➡ *Model*

Joy + Common ➡ *Moment*

My final result of this Beastie Revelation was: *Model + Moment*. Those two words were clues about how I could best show my children I love them, as I'd asked in my original question.

As I sat with those words – *Model and Moment* – I had an

immediate Aha experience: "All I need to do is model for them how to be in the moment. That also puts me in the moment, and being in the moment with them is all I need to do now to show my children I love them."

This realization smacked of truth for me. I felt inspired to get into the moment immediately. I noted that my logical, linear mind might have urged me to do something like take them out to the playground or make cookies for them to show them I love them, but being in the moment with them felt much more right for the time we were all in.

If the results you get from trying out the Beastie Revelation tool seem confusing or unclear to you, set the process aside for a while and come back to it.

Sometimes, it can be helpful to ask a trusted friend to offer their own interpretation of the words that resulted from your free associations. Ask them for their interpretation as if it had been their question and their results. For example, your friend might start by saying, "If this were my Beastie Revelation result, I might think _____." Notice how you react to their ideas, keeping in mind that you're the only one who can know what it means for you. You are the guru in this!

I invite you to send out appreciation and gratitude to the Beasties (or to the universe, or whoever or whatever appeals to you) for pointing you toward this information.

It's perfectly fine to be skeptical about all of this. As one of my teachers told me, "This work is not limited to those who are 'believers.'" The "proof" is only how you feel and what shifts you may experience as you marinate in the results of the Beastie Revelation process. If the results help you feel better or somehow provide helpful insights, then that's your "proof." If not, then that's just fine.

You may find that repeating this process and recording your results lead you to trust in and rely on this process.

In using this practice, you're essentially building a relationship with the Beasties and all that is: the universe, the divine, your higher power. Over time, if you continue to verify for yourself that there's validity in the information you receive, you can use that to deepen your belief and increasingly really *know*, on a cellular level, that there's so much love for you here in these explorations, and that you're unlimited and connected to everything. That's pretty cool.

Shinrin-yoku–The Practice of Forest Bathing

The Japanese term "*shinrin-yoku*" translates as "forest bathing," and is defined as "taking in the forest atmosphere." It's a powerful exercise for connecting to nature and Beastie spirits on a deeper level.

Don't be fooled by the word "forest" in "forest bathing." You can do this practice in any kind of nature. Your backyard. A city park. Beach. Prairie. Marsh. You can do it sitting still in nature or walking through nature at a relaxed pace.

Many scientists are finding evidence that the phytochemicals emitted by plants and trees while we practice activities like forest bathing appear to have healing and enhancing effects on humans. There's so much happening when we're out in nature. It's quite magical and ineffable.

 Pick Your Spot

Find a spot in nature that appeals to you and really draws you in. You can prepare for this by remembering and/or observing what kinds of natural places you're most drawn to – they're often the most powerful places to be in for connecting. I like to call them "thin places" – places where there's not much between us and the world of nature and Beastie energies. It just takes a little contemplation to notice what places feel most inviting to you.

The place you intuitively select will be a powerful place simply because you chose it. Maybe there's a deep forest that invites you. Or you may feel more comfortable in a space that's open and exposed, like a desert, a prairie, or a mountain plateau. Or it might be a corner of your backyard. I know someone who loves to sit under a tree in his backyard in a specific chair and do this exercise.

It can be fabulous to have a place that feels great that's nearby. Then you can return to it whenever you like without a big hassle. But whatever feels good to you is the perfect place.

 Set an Intention

Set an intention of what you'd like to get out of this *shinrin-yoku* time. Are you looking for insight about a particular issue? Is there something you'd like to learn about yourself? Would you like to have a visit from a Guest Beastie to help you with a particular quandary? Or perhaps the intention you want to set is simply to go out and experience joy in nature.

Open All Your Senses

Open all your senses to what's happening around you. Simply take in all the sensory information you can. Either sit in one place or walk at a very relaxed pace that's about 50 percent slower than your normal walking pace.

Doing this for 10 to 30 minutes is a great start. If your mind wanders, that's fine. Just bring it back to what your senses are taking in.

If it's possible, I suggest going barefoot, as that will really enhance the connection to nature and your sensory experience. When was the last time you walked barefoot in nature? You deserve to have that much fun.

 OPEN YOUR EYES

Gaze with soft eyes on what's around you. This soft gaze is often called *wide-angle vision.* Don't focus on anything specific, but open up your vision to extend as far as it can to the right and to the left, up and down, all at once, as far as you easily can. This helps the brain connect to a relaxed state and use its right side, tapping into your intuitive, subconscious self.

What you might see as you do this is evidence of an animal. You may see the path of a deer that's crushed the grass as it headed off into the woods. You may see scat of an animal. You may see a feather or a spider web draped with dew. Any of those kinds of signs point to the presence of a particular Beastie.

 OPEN YOUR EARS

Even though you may never see it, you could hear a woodpecker hammering away on a tree. You may hear squirrels chasing each other in the tree branches above or in the dry leaves below. Perhaps you hear the call of a bird or the buzz of a dragonfly zigging and zagging through the air nearby.

USE YOUR SNIFFER

Encounter this place with your nose. How does it smell? Green and moist, or dry and brittle? Do you smell the natural perfume from blooming trees or fields? What is your nose telling you? Allow your descriptions to be free-form, to come from your right brain. Maybe the air smells yellow or the tree you're leaning against smells like good memories. Just notice the smells and their associations.

NOTICE YOUR SKIN

What sensations are you experiencing via your skin? Does the air feel moist on your bare legs? Does it feel dry? Can you feel bits of sand blowing against your back? Is there a harsh wind? Or is it a very soft breeze? Or is there no wind at all? Do leaves or grasses tickle you as they brush against your arms? How does the earth feel beneath your feet? Is it soft and squishy or firm and unmoving?

 Review Your Experience

Ask yourself what (if any) messages showed up during your forest bathing experience. Were they helpful to you? Was the experience as a whole pleasant? Did anything you experienced suggest a thought or an action to you?

If you came across any Beasties or signs of Beasties while forest bathing, read a bit about them afterwards. If several Beasties showed up, you can pick one that's most interesting to you and read about it first.

You may be surprised how many Beasties you actually become aware of through your various senses as you practice *shinrin-yoku*. I sure was the first time I did it.

Stand still. The trees ahead and the bushes beside you are not lost. The forest breathes. Listen. It answers.

David Wagoner

I invite you to do this exercise as much as possible, to actually make the time for it. The more you do it, the deeper your connection with nature will grow. Keeping a notebook of your *shinrin-yoku* experiences – with the date, your intention, and even a few simple notes about your reflections about what showed up – can be powerful. It can help you begin to define for yourself the most powerful way to practice this *shinrin-yoku* exercise, and it can give you evidence of when the process is working to inform and guide your life. The more we connect with nature, the more magical our lives become.

Choosing a Beastie of the Year

This tool is a wonderful way to celebrate and to set an intention for a new year. I've found that instead of (or in addition to) setting goals to mark the beginning of a new year, selecting a Beastie of the Year is a positive, powerful, and – most importantly – *fun* way to make change happen.
The equation works like this: Intention + Beastie of the Year = Powerful Manifestation.

Choosing a Beastie for the new year can happen anytime – it doesn't only need to be at the start of a new calendar year. For instance, you can chose a Beastie of the year for the time between one birthday and the next.

① Clarify Your Intention
What would be incredibly amazing if it happened in the coming year? What would really make you say, "YES!!!" Starting that

business? Spending more time with friends? Getting amazing feedback from your boss about your performance? Having more romance? Making a big move to somewhere wonderful? Kids who actually listen to you? A long, lean body? Plenty of peace and quiet? Paying off your house? Getting into writing that book? Having tons of energy to do even more of what your heart desires? Getting more downtime and rest to help you enjoy the moments more?

Decide on an intention that really entices you.

EXAMPLE
I intend to shed the activities that are dragging me down so I spend more time working on my writing and being with my kids and my spouse — the things and people that matter most to me.

 Get Specific
What would it take for that intention to come true? What characteristics and qualities would help you really embrace, study, embody, or incorporate that dream into your life?

Ask yourself what three qualities will really assist you.

EXAMPLE
1. Assertiveness
2. Clarity
3. Connection to spirit

 Choose a Beastie Role Model
What Beastie has the qualities you'd like to embrace in this new year as you move toward what you want? Even if you already work with a Core Beastie, this Beastie of the Year process can open up new doorways, ideas, and inspiration through a possible connection with another Beastie that models the

qualities needed as you go after your intention for this year.

Think about the qualities you need to make your intention real? What one Beastie seems to most embody those qualities for you?

Would an ability to rise above the tiny details help you move toward a particular dream this year? That's like taking an eagle's view. Do you want to relax and go with the flow, like a jellyfish? Or to powerfully communicate your desires the way a wolf does? Do you need to step into your power like the fearless dragon? Do you want to accept yourself and love yourself, as does the hedgehog? Do you want to connect with your intuitive gifts, diving deeply like a whale? Or maybe the ant's ability to build amazing structures – one bit of earth at a time – speaks to you about reaching a dream you've clarified. If a dream for the next year will require change and hunting skills, maybe the snake can be a role model, for its ability to shed its skin, renew easily, and taste what's in the air so it can hunt more effectively.

Do you want to connect?

I've learned that every single animal on this planet – from bumblebee to elephant – has something to teach us if we're paying attention. As I write this, I realize that my dog Buttercup certainly has the qualities of peace and focus (especially at mealtimes) down pat.

You can browse through the Manifesto section for ideas about what Beastie might be best for a role model for you for this year. Remember that mythical Beasties (like the dragon, griffin, and unicorn) can also be considered.

EXAMPLE
I chose dragon to help me be assertive and clear. Dragons have fire, can burn through confusion, and are connected to spirit through flight.

explore.
explore.
explore.
explore.
explore.
explore.
explore.
explore.
explore.
xplore.
xplore.
:plore.
plore.
)lore.
)lore.
lore.
:ore.
ore.
)re.
're.
re.
'e.
e.
).

④ Make it Real

Once you've chosen a Beastie of the Year, you can do all sorts of things to invite its help. Just as you would do to honor a Core Beastie, honor your Beastie of the Year in some way. Find playful ways to remember and check in with your Beastie of the Year. Then, when it shows up in your life, pay attention to what's happening ... and be grateful. Gratitude and appreciation seal the deal.

Here are some suggestions for working with a role model Beastie to bring powerful change into your life during the year:

Read all you can about the Beastie you've chosen. Check into any and all resources that excite you to get more information about it. Scan the Beastie Manifestos section in this book to see if your Beastie of the Year is there and, if so, if any of the phrases there resonate for helping you with your intention.

Put a photo, some artistic imagery, or a small figurine in a prominent spot where you'll be reminded daily of your Beastie of the Year. You can also chose a screensaver, doodle an image in your journal, or make a collage to remind you of your Beastie of the Year. Do whatever seems fun and delightful.

Frequently used passwords can also function as reminders of your intention. It makes typing in a password powerful and fun. You can turn your Beastie of the Year into a password, like "Eaglesoarsabove1" or whatever feels right for you. As you enter that password multiple times a day, it will remind you of who you're becoming and what your intention is.

I invite you to explore ways of thanking your Beastie of the Year for being such a fabulous role model. You could honor your

Beastie of the Year by making a donation to an organization that protects it or its habitat, or you could leave an offering for its spirit. For instance, to honor the spirit of a squirrel Beastie of the Year, you could put some sunflower seeds in a special little bowl on a shelf where you'll see it often. Then it becomes a touchstone, reminding you to check in with your Beastie of the Year and give thanks.

As always, as you go about honoring your Beastie of the Year, choose the things to do that sound fantastic to you.

Last night as I was sleeping,

I dreamt—marvelous error! –

that I had a beehive

here inside my heart.

And the golden bees

were making white combs

and sweet honey

from my old failures.

Anotonio Machado

(translation, Robert Bly)

RESOURCE GUIDE

"I thank you God for this most amazing day,
for the leaping greenly spirits of trees,
and for the blue dream of sky and for
everything which is natural,
which is infinite, which is yes."

e.e. cummings

Books

These are some of my favorite books on Beastie symbolism and totems:

Animal-Speak and *Animal-Speak Pocket Guide*
By Ted Andrews

I cannot say enough about the amazing Ted Andrews, who was an incredibly prolific writer and a generous teacher. His book *Animal-Speak* unlocked the world of Beasties for me and I'm forever grateful. His love of his work is so evident in everything he created. He died in 2009, but his spirit lives on.

Totems: The Transformative Power of Your Personal Animal Totem By Brad Steiger

This excellent book offers many unique ways to play with totems, including numerology, melding Beasties with your Zodiac, and saints. I like his unique take on things and his expansive ideas about how to play in this realm.

The Book of Symbols: Reflections on Archetypal Images
By The Archive for Research in Archetypal Symbolism

This beautiful book includes Beastie symbols and many other symbols that are nature-related. This book is stunning, as are all the book published by Taschen (I have a publisher crush!). It looks lovely on a coffee table and is great to keep lying around for fascinating peeks into the deeper meanings of archetypal symbols.

Original Artwork

Artwork by these artists can help you honor your Beastie:

Marian Lansky and Rick Allen

Marian is a digital shaman who transforms vintage, modern, and spiritual graphic elements into brightly colored, evocative works that make me feel happy and hopeful. Her husband Rick's work is hilarious, dark, full of love, and playful. What they do makes my heart explode with joy.
(www.kenspeckleletterpress.com)

Matt Adrian

I love this artist and his work's dark and hilarious sensibilities. He has a book – *It Is Folly to Assume My Awesome Lies Dormant: The Paintings of the Mincing Mockingbird* – of bird paintings that are compelling and moody. The paintings have curious titles based on what the painted bird is "thinking," like "Things best done in a leased Escalade." His products, including original artwork, cards, posters, and prints, can be found on Etsy via his *The Mincing Mockingbird* and *The Frantic Meercat* website.
(www.mincingmockingbird.com)

John Derian

John is famous for his gorgeous decoupage under glass. I have a mad decoupage thing for him and even have a few treasured pieces of his in my house. Many Beasties are featured on his pieces – worth the indulgence! I once tried to foist myself on him at his store in the Bowery in New York. Thank goodness for him he had handlers to keep the kooks away (smile). Visiting with him over a dirty martini someday is a great fantasy of mine. (www.johnderian.com)

Jill Greenberg

In her book *Bear Portraits*, Jill captures majestic bears in stunning, modern images of very coiffed and almost super-naturally beautiful bears. The book includes fabulous, pithy quotes about bears and life. She also has a book of *Monkey Portraits*.

Ravenari

An artist in Perth, Australia, Ravenari ties her beautiful art into her writings about Beasties and their energies. Because of where she is on the globe, she covers some unusual Beasties only found in Australia. (www.wildspeak.com)

Poetry

Poetry can help us connect deeply with the non-ordinary aspect of nature and Beasties. These are some of the poets I've found whose poetry does just that:

Sheila Packa

Sheila writes poems from Lake Superior – the landscape I inhabit. Through her words I experience the wonder and revelations I also get from the world of nature.

Mary Oliver

Just about everything Mary has written seems to connect to nature and Beasties in a most magical way. I'm so glad she decided to throw all of her doors and windows open and share with us what goes on inside her gorgeous heart and mind.

Emily Dickinson

Emily was a shaman tucked away in her quiet cottage. She made wonderful observations of nature and birds.

Nonfiction

Wesley the Owl By Stacey O'Brien

Stacey had an extraordinary relationship with Wesley the owl. This book chronicles their journey through thick and thin, to the bittersweet end. Do keep tissues handy – it's an excellent book if you're need of a grief release.

Kinship with All Life By J. Allen Boone

Written by a Hollywood insider who has some interesting experiences with the Beasties he comes into contact with, this is one of the most elegant and profound collections of Beastie-connection stories I know of. It's funny, insightful, and brilliant.

The Sound of a Wild Snail Eating By Elisabeth Tova Baily

This is a memoir of a woman bedridden by a baffling illness. Her belief in possibilities is rekindled by a single wild snail who takes up residence next to her bed. Her story beautifully illustrates the power of one tiny Beastie's spirit to change everything.

Elephantoms: Tracking the Elephant By Lyall Watson

This book is all about the magical relationship between elephants, a boy, and a man. Lyall was raised in a time when boys were allowed to live dangerously and that was a very good thing. If you love elephants, I recommend that you drop everything and read this book right now.

The Wolf in the Parlor By Jon Franklin

A fascinating scientific expedition into the evolution of dogs, told as a parallel story with the author's healing relationship with a poodle. If you're interested in neuroscience and dogs, you'll love this book.

Shamanism

Here are resources to help with diving deeper into shamanism:

The Foundation for Shamanic Studies
The Foundation offers classes, workshops, and other resources. Their programs are geared toward helping Westerners regain their "spiritual heritage." (www.shamanism.org)

Timothy Cope
Timothy is an instructor in shamanic practice in the Midwest. He's a phenomenal teacher — powerful and irreverent (my favorite combination for an instructor). He teaches workshops all over the Midwest. If you live in or near Minneapolis, you're in luck, as Timothy does a regular drumming circle there for shamanic journeying. (www.rattledrum.com)

Awakening to the Spirit World: The Shamanic Path of Direct Revelation By Sandra Ingerman and Hank Wesselman
This primer on shamanism draws on the collective wisdom of several major players in the North American shamanic scene. It includes a CD for shamanic journeying.

Shamanic Meditations: Guided Journeys for Vision, Insight, and Healing By Sandra Ingerman
This CD is a marvelous collection of recordings that serves as an introduction to the world of shamanic journeying. Sandra is a very comforting and loving presence to have along if you chose to dive into this adventure.

Seeing in the Dark: Claim Your Own Shamanic Power Now and in the Coming Age **By Colleen Deatsman & Paul Bowersox**
I wish I'd found this book earlier than I did. Colleen and Paul have a powerful way of writing – their book explains the basics of shamanism well, in a way that's essential and effective.

The Way of the Shaman **By Michael Harner**
Michael was compelled to take what he learned in the jungles and bring it to a larger audience in North America. This classic text is technical and lays a good foundation for the practice. The section on Ayuasca journeys may make you think you'd never want to go on a shamanic journey (smile) … but don't let it stop you. Do go on a journey via drumming if you're interested in trying it out.

Shapeshifting into Higher Consciousness: Heal and Transform Yourself and Our World with Ancient Shamanic and Modern Methods **By Llyn Roberts**
This author has a wonderful way of describing what it means to shapeshift, she makes it accessible.

Further Fun Delights

Oils and Essences
Beastie spirits love a little alluring scent. Using oils and essences is a great way to honor your Beastie and play with stepping into your wolf or black mamba snake. An amazing resource for this is Lynx Graywolf's collection of essences. Lynx is a shaman who writes beautifully about many different Beasties and her own interpretations of their energies. Check out her "Animal/

Shamanic Essence" collection by going to the link below and scrolling down. I often share these essences with people when I take groups on journeys, and they get rave reviews. (http://morningstar.netfirms.com/essences.html)

Virtual Vision Board

On the Pinterest website, you can create a virtual "pinboard" to honor your Beastie. My hunch is that many of us who are drawn to Beastie and totem work are eidetic thinkers – we think in images. A fun way to honor a Beastie is to create a collection of images dedicated to it. Pinterest makes this easy to do digitally. You can update and visit your collection whenever you want to connect with Beastie energies and strengths. (www.pinterest.com)

iPhone App

Animal Totem is an iPhone app by August Hesse. It's a good guide for on-the-go totem interpretations and divinations. This is an excellent app to use for sharing the idea of totems with friends. My teenager once did a divination at dinner, using this app to discover a Core Beastie, and got the same family of Beasties *six times in a row* – so statistically impossible it's ridiculous. Which just goes to show that there are no accidents if your intention is clear and you desire to receive helpful information. (http://itunes.apple.com/ca/app/animal-totem/id306635565?mt=8)

It is far better to have a firm anchor in nonsense than to put out

on the troubled seas of thought.

John Kenneth Gailbraith

BEASTIE MANIFESTOS

"Hello Beastie!"

Captain Jack Sparrow

Manifestos – There's a Zoo in You

I wrote each of these Beastie Manifestos by drawing on a vast constellation of sources, including (but not limited to) hard science resources; children's natural history guides from the late 1800s to early 1900s; trips to South Africa, Utah, California, and Arizona; and (whenever possible) my own direct experiences, which include Beastie encounters in ordinary physical reality, dreams, shamanic journeys, explorations of pop culture, films, nonfiction works about Beasties studied closely by humans, and input from the many amazing individuals who work directly with Beastie energies and have generously shared their experiences with me.

THE SIGNIFICANCE OF A BEASTIE THAT APPEARS IN YOUR LIFE IS LEFT IN YOUR HANDS

The significance or meaning for you of each Guest Beastie or Core Beastie that appears in your life is best left in your hands. These Manifestos are meant to be helpful as jumping-off points.

Our buoyancy is very useful when exploring the realms of the Beasties in our lives, especially when we're approaching Beasties that, at first encounter, may bring up in us a reaction of fear or rejection. Because of that, in these Manifestos you'll find many interjections of lightness and love. Notably missing are shadow elements or negative implications – not because I don't think it's useful to examine the dark side (feel free to do so), but because I've found that many of the more daring, creative, maverick change agents and eccentrics (like you and me) powerfully benefit from a positive spin.

I invite you to play with these Manifestos literally and metaphorically. Take what you like and leave the rest. Notice what tastes of truth for you. The truth always tastes of freedom. And freedom is good. Very good.

Domestic Beasties are omitted from the Manifestos, but because pets may be portals for getting into working with wild Beasties, you can check out a wild version of a pet if you're drawn to that idea (for example, if you're a dog lover, check out the wolf Manifesto).

The number of Manifestos here doesn't begin to comprehensively cover the vast world of Beastie variety. I chose Beasties to include in the Manifestos based on which ones I feel need to be included, are particularly dear to me, and are least understood. I believe each Beastie, like each human, is born to realize its own greatness and is imbued with the potential to create whatever is desired. The Manifestos are written in this spirit.

As Beasties show up in your life and as you consult the Manifestos about them, take note of your impressions. See for yourself if racking up your own experiences as evidence helps you move deeper and more meaningfully into the world of the Beasties. Everyone who opens up to this world and listens is already a little bit shaman.

Above all, I hope you enjoy!

enjoy! enjoy! enjoy! enjoy! enjoy! enjoy! enjoy! enjoy! enjoy! enjoy! enjoy! enjoy! enjoy! enjoy! enjoy! enjoy! enjoy! enjoy! enjoy enjoy enjo' enjo enjo enj en; en en e e e

BEASTIE

manifesto contents

BEASTIE

manifesto contents

BADGER
manifesto

FAVOR FLEXIBILITY
Hang loose. Make like water and stay fluid.

EMBRACE DESIRE
Surrender to what you love. Commit whole-heartedly.

EASY PEASY
You've got it. Strut it. Wow 'em.

PERSEVERANCE PAYS OFF
Go beyond. Go further. Complete the mission.

BELIEVE IN BOUNTY
Need it? Take it. There's always more.

BUST THROUGH
Find your second wind. Your inner warrior. For what matters.

WEATHER THE WOUNDS
Is it worth fighting for? Then breathe through the sting.

EXPEND ... THEN MEND
Even a badass needs to heal and recover.

FOCUS
Remember why. Dig in.

DEVIATE TO DISCOVER
Ignore everyone. Innovate.

BAT
manifesto

EMBODY MEMORIES
Remember kinesthetically. Be the map home.

AVOID OBSTACLES
Swoop. Dodge and dart. Navigate naturally.

BE UNIQUELY VISIONARY
See what others can't. Perceive depths. Lead the way.

PURSUE ASKEW
Upside down. Backwards. Whatever it takes to feel good.

SENSE WHAT'S OUT THERE
Reach with your sensitive skills. Find. Capture.

BALANCE MULTI-DIMENSIONALLY
Redefine equilibrium. Both yin and yang. Defy categories.

REVIEW YOUR REPERTOIRE
Come in at an unexpected angle. Arrive via your best path.

ROOST TO REFILL
Congregate. Hang out. Keep each other warm as you yammer.

ACT WITH COURAGE
Fight for what matters. To you. To those you care about.

LISTEN
Suspend everything for a moment. Focus in. Amplify.

DREAM DEEPLY

BEAR
manifesto

DREAM DEEPLY
Clamber into your cave to roam without limits.

GO YOUR OWN WAY
Find strength in solitude. Discover alone.

INTUIT TIME
Prepare. You'll recognize the right moment to release.

SAVOR THE AMBLE
Find delight in the journey. Stop often for honey.

KNOW TO SLOW
Conserve. Build reserves for downtime.

DIG IN
Expose. Examine. Find nourishment.

SCAMPER TO A VIEW
Gain perspective. Look around. Adjust as needed.

FEAST ON LIFE
Delight in the cornucopia. What whets your appetite? Go there.

EXPECT YOUR CREATIONS TO THRIVE
You did your part. Now let go. Be fierce. Believe.

SCRATCH THE ITCH
Give in to delight. Indulge your heart's desire.

— BEAVER —
manifesto

HONOR SELF
Keep faith with your values. Clamp on. Adhere.

CREATE MEANINGFULLY
Hatch a plan. Why do it? Use why to deepen purpose.

RETREAT INTO BEAUTY
Dream into being. Savor your lovely creation.

PROCESS RAW MATERIALS
What's nearby? Examine. Re-work. Enjoy the process.

ENGAGE DAILY
Commit to the high vision, but do what's next today.

DEPEND ON HOME
Delight in your environment. Tailor it. Let it ground you.

KEEP IT COZY
Maintain. Beautify. Invest. Lavish with care.

ADJUST THE FLOW
Direct energy thoughtfully. Calm turbulence. Create peace.

BEFRIEND FORCE
Work smart. Lighten your load. Travel easily from A to B.

DIG DOWN
Go below. Deeper. Explore until satisfied. Expose the hidden.

flow. 'low. low. low. ow. ow. ow. 'w. w. v.

BUFFALO
manifesto

CONSERVE OOMPH
Energy is currency. Use it wisely. Choose when.

MOVE UNPREDICTABLY
Follow a feeling to a different path. No need to explain.

CHOOSE CHAMPIONS
Hang with worthy pals. Benefits abound.

LET GO
It's all easy. Harness hidden forces and go with the flow.

TAKE UP SPACE
Wander. Find room to roam. Remain unconfined.

MULL IT OVER
Chew things over. Revise. Find the nourishment.

KEEP GOING
Stay in your zone. Determination trumps all.

BE MAJESTIC
Claim it. Own it. With grace in each step.

BARREL ON THROUGH
Connect with your inner freight train.

GRAZE
Browse and pick. It all adds up.

BUTTERFLY
manifesto

USE ALCHEMY
Spin self into gold. Create anew.

MELT DOWN
Become liquid. Rearrange. Soul knows how.

IGNITE
Become still. Then explode into the sky.

FLIT
Allow distraction. Alight on ideas. Combine.

FAN JOY
Be the magic. Land unexpectedly. Manifest inner smiles.

KNOW WITHOUT KNOWING
Check deep inside. Find truth. Trust.

SAY YES TO MESS
Relax in disorder. What needs to get done will.

FROLIC FREELY
Bounce where your heart takes you. Explore bliss.

ACT NOW
In this brief flash. This moment. And this.

GO ETERNAL
Never-ending. Ever-present. Unhurried. Unworried.

    sarah bamford seidelmann m.d. | www.whatthewalrusknows.com

CAMEL (WILD)

manifesto

THRIVE
Where solitude lives. In good company.

HABITS HELP
Routines conserve energy and resources.

ADORE
Kneel at the foot of love. Even if challenging.

BE DIRECT
Get there faster. Say what you mean. Be non-deviant.

DEPEND ON YOUR DESIGN
Protection is built in. Assume positions others can't. Go ahead.

FIND STRENGTH IN SERVICE
What's mine is yours. No I. Only we. And we're connected.

STEADY NOW
Surefooted in shifting conditions. One foot in front of the other.

ENDURE
Enjoy the wild ride. Bump along. Go the distance.

RELY ON RESERVES
Of energy. Of abundance. Of love. Especially of love.

DEPEND ON THE DREAM STATE
Connect with deeper messages. Create anew. Become willing.

COYOTE

manifesto

GOAD
Nudge. Poke. Get them on their feet. Goose 'em good.

SAY IT
Remove the filter. Don't hold back. Express freely.

CONVINCE WITH CLEVERNESS
Guide with guile. Win with wiles. (They'll thank you later.)

KEEP IT UP
Zero in on your passion. Track with unstoppable stamina.

FEED YOUR CREATION
Nurture with extra care. Get help if needed.

BELONG TO A TRIBE
One you love and respect. Work together. Dream together.

BE LOYAL
Commit wholeheartedly. Savor and honor the depth of your ties.

PRIORITIZE PARTNERSHIP
Recognize communion's benefits. Celebrate unions.

INDULGE INNOCENCE
Yours and theirs. Cavort childishly. View anew.

PUSH THE ENVELOPE
Reach beyond what's expected. Or even possible.

CROW
manifesto

ROOST COMMUNALLY
Collect companions. Compare. Share. Refuel.

NOTICE
Find magic in the ordinary. Resources are in plain view.

COLLECT WHAT GLITTERS
Snatch up treasures. Examine. Use to create pleasure.

TOUCH GROUND
See what's right in front of you. Deal with that. Love it.

TAKE FLIGHT
Soar above. Leverage perspective. Devise a strategy.

INTRIGUE
Don't let their judgment distract you. Be magically mysterious.

BE COURAGEOUS
Take the plunge. Action alerts magical forces.

EMPLOY YOUR INTELLECT
Wield your noggin. Crack the problem. Invent.

BELIEVE UNSEEN FORCES
Awareness expands to encompass all. Ask for help.

PLAY WITH POWER
Use it for great good. Learn to bend the universe.

DEER

manifesto

VAMOOSE
Retreat. Fade. Disappear. Your senses tell you when.

EYES WIDE OPEN
Notice beauty everywhere. Hidden in plain sight.

GO WITH GRACE
Transform the ordinary into the rarified.

LEAP INTO LOVE
Open your heart. Always with compassion.

SEE WITHOUT SEEING
Open all channels. Sense exquisitely. Detect subtleties others miss.

QUIETLY CONVINCE
Stand in power. Your presence transforms others.

MEDITATE ON THIS MOMENT
Awareness transforms. Every time. Forever.

WELCOME INNOCENCE
Be like a child again. At play in the grass. Unafraid.

SHARE WHAT'S MOST TENDER
With those who can hear. The lovely ones. The wild ones.

DISCOVER NEW ROUTES
To create. To uncover the hidden. For thrill and delight.

DOLPHIN
— manifesto —

SURRENDER TO EFFERVESCENCE
Cavort. Get carried away. In joy. In play.

GLIDE BEAUTIFULLY
Over and under the surface. Move in gorgeousness.

STIR IT UP
Spin up the mud. Let the heavy stuff sink. Discover clarity.

SING YOUR SONG
Bask in your music. Tune your message. Send it out to the universe.

DIG HIJINKS
Leap for joy. Because you can. Binge on levity.

SWIM WITH THE SHARKS
Navigate with joy and charge with heart.

EXHALE WITH FORCE
Unleash into empty space. Savor. Enjoy the tantric interlude.

INDULGE YOUR INNER WAG
What sounds fun? Make mischief. Invite gleeful pals along.

SWAY AND BEND
Dance is an approach. Use every cell. Feel the flex.

FIND SOME FROTH
Slip into bliss. Share it with the pod.

glide. glid glid glid gli gli gl gl g

DRAGON
manifesto

LOVE LUXURY
What catches your eye? Hunt and gather. Curate beauty.

TEND YOUR LAIR
Layer with treasures. Bask in what you adore.

SHARE THE WEALTH
Spread abundance when you love. Do it for you.

DREAM WITHOUT LIMITS
Dive into your inner vision. Home in on the amazing.

CAVORT TO CONVINCE
Goof off to attract. Invite fun. Entice to empower.

BREATHE FIRE
Use your voice to transform. Ignite through expression.

SEEK A UNIQUE PERSPECTIVE
From the ground. Mid-flight. Mountaintop. Shift it.

WATCH FOR SIGNS
Study clouds. Which way does the wind blow? Intuit meaning.

SOAR TO RESTORE
Your power. A connection. Open your wings to all that is.

GRAB OPPORTUNITY
Take power. Don't wait. And use it well.

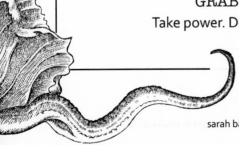

sarah bamford seidelmann m.d. | www.whatthewalrusknows.com

DRAGONFLY
manifesto

PILOT WITH PANACHE
Dive. Hover. Zoom. No move is too flashy.

TWIST AND TURN
Take a roundabout route. Enjoy a zig and a zag. For fun.

EMBRACE INFINITY
Merge past and present. Transform. Melt down and be reborn.

HOME IN ON BEAUTY
Loveliness is everywhere. Not everyone can see it. You can.

TAKE IN A WIDE VIEW
See the whole panorama from multiple angles.

SPEED TO THE SCENE
You are a racing stripe. Embody velocity.

SOOTH THE TROUBLED
Make yourself known. Alight with peace. All is well.

REFLECT
Shine like a jewel in the mirror of the lake. See yourself.

REUNITE
Fly together. Fly apart. Reconnect. Do a parallel dance.

BE POWERFULLY SUPERNATURAL
Arise from magic. Be magic. Make your own magic.

EAGLE

manifesto

SOAR CEREMONIOUSLY
Harness currents. Rest above it all. Enjoy the view.

OVERSEE STRATEGY
Get the mile-high view. Take your vision to those on the ground.

CONSERVE VERVE
Expend judiciously. When it matters most.

RESPECT POWER TOOLS
Handle with care. With love. With respect. To awaken.

USE THE FORCE GRANDLY
Do the right thing. Take what's yours. Set limits.

TRAVEL TO REFUEL
Feed your soul. Discover spirit. Connect with power.

OPPORTUNITY ABOUNDS
Choose what fulfills. Affirm life.

MAGNETIZE
Envision. Draw in what you love.

SEEK QUALITY
Rarified. Heavenly. Extraordinary.

ACTION SHOWS PASSION
Sky-dance. Dive. Ascend. Create. Nurture.

ELEPHANT
manifesto

FAMILY IS EVERYTHING
Choose them. Use them. Never lose them.

PATIENCE SERVES LOVE
Now is infinite. So is hope.

MESSY IS A METHOD
Throw stuff around. Find the prize sooner.

SHOW YOUR HEART
Cry easily. Lament. Forgive.

RELY ON YOUR POSSE
Rally the troops. Get some buddy bravery.

GRACE IS AN ATTITUDE
Size is immaterial. Lift your chin. Waltz.

CLEAR A PATH FOR YOURSELF
Own your strength. Use it to move it.

CREATE A RUMPUS
Kick up some dust. Act the fool. Romp.

THROW YOUR WEIGHT AROUND
Take up space. Be your own bouncer.

SENSITIVITY IS AN ASSET
Use your sniffer. Tune in to tune up.

FOX

manifesto

FOCUS KEENLY
Turn awareness on. Home in. Recognize solutions.

BE INEFFABLE
Neither here nor there. Betwixt, between, and beyond. Unknown.

VAPORIZE
Melt magically. Rearrange. Disappear and reappear elsewhere.

REMAIN TRUE
Anchor in essence. Remember. Merge and re-create.

GOOF OFF
Take a dose of nonsense. For medicinal purposes.

ASSIMILATE BIT BY BIT
A little here. A little there. Abundance. Love. It adds up.

MESMERIZE
Maximize unique skills, like stealth and poetic dance.

EXPOSE TRUTH
What is real? Find the piece. And the peace.

BEFRIEND INNOCENCE
Keep it company. Play in its arena. Guard it.

UNLEASH SURPRISE
Enjoy being nonconformist. Draw on your inner multitude.

66 Above all, watch with glittering eyes
the whole world around you, because the
greatest secrets are always hidden in the
most unlikely places. Those who don't
believe in magic will never find it. 99

Roald Dahl

FROG

—— manifesto ——

POUNCE ON BOUNTY
Grab delight swiftly. Appreciate in a split-second.

LIVE IN HARMONY
Tune the tribe. Bring balance to community.

MASTER CHANGE
Allow the old to fall away. Move into new birth.

PLUNGE INTO DREAMING
Know where you want to go. Follow the flow. Swim in.

CROAK WITH GUSTO
Sing your own eccentric song. Draw in those who can hear.

COLLECT THE UNCONVENTIONAL
Seek non-conformists. Make pals with bohemians.

BE VERSATILE
Embrace flexibility. Stretch. Reach. Return to center.

NOTICE THE NEW
Opportunities. Updated abilities. Fresh ways to move forward.

LIE LOW
Blending in amplifies opportunity. Scan and notice.

SAFEGUARD CREATIONS
Provide shelter. Away from commotion. Let them grow in peace.

pounce.
pounce.
pounce.
pounce.
pounce.
pounce.
pounce.
pounce.
pounce.
pounce.
pounce.
pounce.
pounce.
pounce.
pounce.
ounce.
unce.
unce.
unce.
nce.
nce.
nce.
ce.
ce.
ce.
e.
e.

GIRAFFE

manifesto

IMPROVISE
Release your inner thespian. Act out to renew.

SHARE YOUR VISION
Look ahead. Let others know what you see.

FULL THROTTLE AHEAD
Sprint. So what if it's awkward. Leave 'em in the dust.

OWN YOUR WOW FACTOR
Supernatural. Fantastical. Turn some heads.

USE EVERYTHING
In trouble? Sway. Wobble. Kick. Channel power all ways.

LEVERAGE THE LOVE
Everyone helps. Give. Receive. Depend. Deserve.

SAFEGUARD THE TENDER
Protect. Conceal. Reveal with care.

FOLD SAFELY
Judge well. Then sink into vulnerability.

TAKE YOUR PICK
Feast high. Graze low. Reach.

NATURALLY GOOD-NATURED
Amiable. Kind. Keeper of the peace.

HIPPOPOTAMUS

manifesto

DEFY DESCRIPTION
Exist outside the box. Baffle. Be terribly unexpected.

GET BUOYANT
Lightness brings ease. Rise up. Giggle.

BLISS OUT
Enjoy small pleasures. Toes sunk into sand. Cool water.

SUBMERGE
Explore underneath. Pop up to assess. Peek. Retreat.

VARY THE SETTING
Walk the river bottom. Graze the land. Get what you need.

DEFEND YOUR CLAIM
Guard aggressively. Chase away the disrespectful.

BELLOW IN CAHOOTS
Snort. Grunt. Roar. Create a lively tumult together.

LEVERAGE READINESS
Rest while wide awake. Plunge quickly at opportunity.

MAKE MISCHIEF
Frolic fuels creation. Initiate high-spirited shenanigans.

GLIDE SKILLFULLY
Advance gracefully. Peaceful forward motion is an art.

HONEY BADGER
manifesto

EMBRACE DESIRE
Surrender. Commit. Throw everything you've got at what you love.

BE FLEXIBLE
Hang loose. Make like water and stay fluid.

THIS IS EASY!
They'll ogle. And gasp. You're so adept it's scary.

STAY FOCUSED
Keep going. Stick to it. Whatever it takes.

COUNT ON BOUNTY
Take what's needed. Leave what's not. Teach others how it's done.

SURRENDER
Breathe into it. Pain is transmuted. Honey will flow.

FAILURE IS NOT THE END
Rest. Restore. Heal. Go back to being bad-ass.

FINISH
Remember why you began. Re-focus. Complete your mission.

INNOVATE
Go where others don't. Ignore them all. No comparison.

DETACH
Let go of their opinions. Pursue passions with reckless abandon.

* This Manifesto is dedicated to Randall, of YouTube video fame.

HORSE (WILD)
manifesto

GO FULL THROTTLE
Burst into speed. Tap your endurance.

WHEEL AROUND
Curve and swerve. Adjust the trajectory. Change course.

PAY ATTENTION
Let energy lead. What feels good next? Go there.

BREAK NEW GROUND
The world is a playground. Explore. Gain experience.

PINPOINT THE POSSE
Maintain connections. Stay close to your companions.

FIND A HOLE IN THE FENCE
Run because you can. Open wide. Wider.

WATCH OUT
Wait for the signal. When the time is right, rush and plunge.

CAVORT AND SNORT
Unleash silliness. Get wacky. Let off steam. Play to clear your head.

CHANNEL ENERGY
Get mystical. Practice. Use wisely. Use often.

REMAIN UNTAMED
You have your own ways. You are enough.

HUMMINGBIRD
manifesto

LIGHT UP
Set your desire on fire. Be big passion in a small package.

EMBODY BOLDNESS
Dive on desire with courage. Take charge.

INDULGE
Drink in what's lovely. Beauty feeds and recharges.

BE DISCERNING
View from all angles. Hover. Carefully land on what feels best.

MASTER THE FORCE
High octane output requires quality input. Stay well-fueled.

ZERO IN ON SUGAR
Target sweet spots. Use your intuitive radar.

VARY THE SOURCE
Dig in. Taste. Combine. Try it all. Invent something new.

FETCH FEROCIOUSLY
Seize on behalf of your heart. Capture essence. Share it.

RETURN TO THE HEART
Revisit reliable sources. Trust. Rest.

TURN DOWN THE FURNACE
Seriously slack off. Mentally and physically. Return to core.

JAGUAR
manifesto

ROAM IN RAPTURE
Wander. Explore densely perfumed areas. Search.

INVESTIGATE THOROUGHLY
Get a 360-degree view. Study. Drink in all the details.

PROWL WITH TEETH
Own your strength. Realize what's possible.

EXPRESS YOURSELF
Free your voice. Let loose. To thrill and ignite.

DEFINE BOUNDARIES
Stake out your territory. Leave signatures and signposts.

WAIT...THEN SPRINT
Patience. Small advances. Get close. Then become the arrow.

RACE AFTER FUN
Chase delight with delight. Be the surprise.

GO SOLO
Endeavor to be alone. Prefer to be reserved.

CHOOSE REFUGE
Step up out of view. Recharge. Retreat to a higher plane.

HEED THE CALL
Accept the hero's journey. Accept help along the way

LION

manifesto

SHARE GOALS
Rally the troops. Decide who'll lead. Share duty and reward.

PATIENCE PAYS
Be willing to wait. Pounce when inspired.

DEFEND WITH FEROCITY
Claim what's yours. Let no one get in your way.

FOSTER AFFECTION
As glue for family bonds. To heal and strengthen.

SLEEP IN A HEAP
Surrender to gravity. Drape. Snuggle. Yawn.

STUDY STILLNESS
Open your senses. Sniff the breeze. Breathe in the moment.

LIVE THE LEGEND
Full of fire and light. Aglow. Luminous. Incandescent.

SPEAK WITH SUBTLETY
Use body language. Expand the vocabulary. Experiment with pitch

MANAGE ENERGY
Go full throttle. Then rest deeply. Repeat.

FORGE BONDS
Togetherness keeps you strong.

MANATEE

manifesto

FEED YOUR APPETITE
Be naturally voracious. Indulge. Then rest.

SHIELD YOUR VIBE
Protect your powers. Seek peace.

RECHARGE CONTINUOUSLY
Go motionless. Float. Snuggle in.

LINGER TO ENLIVEN
Dally. Find quiet, hidden spots. Restore your spirit.

MINIMIZE EFFORT
Everything is within easy reach. Allow simplicity.

CAPTIVATE THE AUDIENCE
Allure. Mystify. Appear splendidly out of nowhere.

BE DEVOTION IN MOTION
Surrender to love's flow. Connect and nurture.

DANCE YOUR DANCE
Perform a ballet of surprising grace. Personal. Perfect.

DECLARE WITH DETERMINATION
Be specific. Calm. Quiet. Yet firm.

HOLD YOUR POSITION
Budge only if it feels right. Otherwise, maintain.

MEERKAT
manifesto

STAND IN COURAGE
Know what you want. Go get it. Let your brave heart lead.

CHECK PERIPHERIES FOR EPIPHANIES
What's waiting in the wings? At the edges? Scan 360 degrees.

DIG FOR GOODIES
Find delights under the surface. Even in the darkest places.

GRAZE FOR NOURISHMENT
Little bites here and there. Bit by bit. To satisfaction.

MULTIPLY POWER
Higher and faster. Supercharged. Zoom your path.

CELEBRATE CREATIONS
Show 'em off. Invite the village. Awe the crowd.

CULTIVATE YOUR TEAM
Raise the tribe's energy. Play to their strengths. And yours.

LEAVE TO LEAD
Sometimes moving on benefits everyone. Watch for signs.

LAVISH LEARNING
Amplify your repertoire. Teach. Pass on a gift of knowledge.

ROTATE RESPONSIBILITY
Take the helm. Then switch and row. Cooperation is best.

MONKEY
manifesto

FOLLOW CURIOSITY
Quest. Examine. Touch. Discover.

WATCH CLOSELY
Observe others. What works? Try it. Break through.

IMPROVISE
Feel your way. Act as if. Leap from idea to idea.

CLIMB UP
Study the horizon. See what's coming. Seek opportunities.

NURTURE SENSUALITY
Give and receive. Snuggle. Affection connects. Make it a habit.

IMMERSE IN CULTURE
Tribal and individual. Appreciate nuances. Recognize universality.

RESPECT STRUCTURE
Support order. Rely and contribute. Everyone benefits.

TRUST THE SCOUTS
Relax and let them alert, guide, and protect.

ACT ON HUNCHES
What do you crave? Investigate angles. Remain unattached.

PLAY DAILY
Find the time. Break free of the construct. Let go.

MOOSE

manifesto

ENJOY YOUR OWN SHOW
Show up. Let them all have a good look. Make a striking impression.

BE NIMBLE
Twinkle-toed. Stable in tight spots. Where others can't tread.

EXPLOIT AWKWARDNESS
Unwieldy gives way to grace. Get out there. Make mistakes.

VEER SHARPLY
Engage abrupt change. Turn on a dime when it feels right.

HEED THE CALL
What speaks to you? Listen. Wander towards. Connect with power.

ENGAGE PASSION
Exploit urges. Channel the energy to create. Don't wait. Ignite.

LOVE HATH FURY
Stake your claim. Defend. Chase off unhelpful influences.

SWIM OUT
To wonder. To what intrigues you. To solitude.

UNLEASH YOUR INNER JACKASS
Let the silly flow. Practice makes for perfect fun.

FALLING IN LINE ALIGNS
Listen for your tribe. Follow. Or lead.

www.whatthewalrusknows.com | sarah bamford seidelmann m.d.

MOUSE
manifesto

BE LEGENDARY
Goodness multiplied. Ideas in abundance.

DIG SOFTNESS
Use whatever you have. Process it. Muffle out the noise.

SLIGHT IS MIGHT
The tweaks. The leverage. The tipping point.

PLAY IT LOOSE
Allow the good to flow. Through you. To the world.

GOBBLE IT UP
Satisfy your hunger. Sustain yourself. Body and soul.

PROFIT FROM OBSCURITY
Seek hidden places. Delve in darkness. Tend your own fire.

SCAMPER PURPOSEFULLY
Quietly pursue. What matters. What needs doing.

EXPLORE CRANNIES
Discoveries abound. Right under their noses. Imagination steers.

SCURRY AWAY
To freedom. To a better place. With the wise and gentle.

BE TENACIOUS
Incline towards desire. Focus. Hold.

OCTOPUS
manifesto

ENJOY WITHOUT FEAR
Identify desire. Hold on loosely. Let it unfold.

CATCH AND RELEASE
As needed, set others free. To go, do, be what they must.

HEART, HEAD, SOUL
Connect with heart. Lead with head. Inject soul.

FIND COMFORT IN CONFINEMENT
Limits show the way. Make the most of what is.

EPITOMIZE FLOW
Go boneless. Que sera. Revel without resistance.

HIDE IN PLAIN VIEW
Become one with all. Be the veil. Sway. Lift.

KEEP YOUR TOOLS HANDY
Simple is best. Infuse with your spirit. Wield often.

DIRECT WITH CARE
Identify what's crucial. Show others so they can integrate.

DIGEST DREAMS
Remember. Ask. Discover great counsel.

DELIGHT IN SYMMETRY
Find ease in balance. All things are equal.

OTTER
manifesto

FLEXIBILITY IS EASE
You cannot make a wrong turn.

PLAY TO LEARN
Be willing to fail. Engage fully to become the best.

SENSE PLEASURE
Share delights. Invite others to sun, enjoy, and cuddle.

EXERT FIERCENESS
Let others know you're in charge. No exceptions.

USE BUDDY POWER
Hang out to recharge. Stay connected. Delight in each other.

SHOW THEM HOW
Demonstrate. Expect participation. Ask them to teach another.

SHOO FOR YOU
Everybody out! Now, do what you need to do.

APPRECIATE ENTANGLEMENT
Immersion. Suspension. Unraveling.

REST TO MANIFEST
Allow yourself to float. Create. Receive.

OPEN UP
Heal your wounds. Let love in. Be a warrior of the heart.

OWL

manifesto

POUNCE JOYFULLY
Dive-bomb what draws you. For the thrill. With a loop-de-loop.

TRY AGAIN
When you crash, arise. Open back up. Become willing.

SURPRISE WITH LOVE
Sneak in. Swoop silently onto what your heart longs for.

GET LARGE
Show them your strength. Let them flinch.

INHALE IT ALL
Take in what you need. Let the rest go.

DEVOTE YOURSELF
Partner on an intimate scale. Love to the power of two.

EVADE ROUTINE
Sleep all day. Work all night. Find your groove.

KEEP YOUR OWN COUNSEL
Wisdom is cellular. And sensed in the wind. You just know.

MAKE IT VISIBLE
See every angle. Illuminate their blind side. Spotlight truth.

BEFRIEND ENDINGS
Allow things to fall apart. Grieve. Let go. Begin anew.

POLAR BEAR
manifesto

WALK AWAY
Steal a moment. An hour. A week. A season.

THRIVE AS ONE
Find strength in self-sufficiency. You're free to flourish.

POLISH IT OFF
The effort is worth it. Take it to the finish line.

DIVE IN
Use your buoyancy to glide. Get in the swim. Dream deeply.

AMUSE YOURSELF
Find a toy. Make up a game. Play is paramount.

PERSONALIZE THE SEASONS
Watch the wind. Take stock. Hunker down. Emerge anew.

TRUST BREATH
Rely on the rhythm. Inhale. Recharge. Exhale. Pursue.

PLOD
Set a leisurely pace. No rush. Everything is already present.

ENVISION A BIG FUTURE
Indulge your imagination. Let it play. Protect it.

BLEND IN TO STAND OUT
Follow your true path. Calmly. Those who need to see you will.

PORCUPINE
manifesto

LIVE AT LEISURE
Casually close in on desires. Unhurried. No worries.

GO OUT ON A LIMB
Reach for it. Put yourself out there. Take a chance.

BE SALTY
Of the earth. Down to earth. Savoring truth.

STAND YOUR GROUND
No threats needed. Your true power is visible.

SEEK TREATS
A taste. A smell. A touch. Enjoy daily.

CONCEIVE ARTFULLY
Bring something entirely new into realty.

RENEW COURAGE
Decide. Change your mind. Decide again. Move forward.

FOLLOW SUBTLE FEELINGS
Guard your unique gifts of sensitivity. Tune up. Tune in.

GO BETWIXT
Locate the magic between extremes. Create there.

BE MULTIFACETED
Nice? Yes. Adorable? Sometimes. Pushover? Hell, no!

No. 144

RABBIT
manifesto

HARNESS HARDINESS
Thrive on challenge. Go the distance. Bring it.

NAVIGATE SENSUALLY
Get quiet. Tune in. Leap if you feel it. Be still if not.

MASTER VELOCITY
Zoom. Grab the lead. Get there first.

SHAPESHIFT
Disguise. Blend. Become one with everything.

UNLEASH CREATIVITY
Free up ideas. Select what sings to you. Let the others go.

COMPANIONS CALM CHAOS
Get gregarious. Discover new fields together.

STRATEGIZE
Back up. Switch lanes. Do the unexpected.

BE HERE NOW
Nowhere better. No time better. Guaranteed.

REFUEL IN BATTLE
Take a time-out between rounds. Then relaunch.

HAVEN IS HEAVEN
Retreat to home. Bask. Lapse into peace

"Enter the day invigorated with the essence of possibility, go through it energized with a sense of purpose and joy and end it with the serenity of completion."

Darina Stoyanova

RACOON
manifesto

BE NIMBLE AND QUICK
You have this. Scramble up on top. It's easy.

MAKE MISCHIEF
Titillate devilishly. Channel a bit of madness. For fun.

MAXIMIZE YOUR CHARISMA
You have it. Use it. Intrigue. With intent.

ALLURE ENIGMATICALLY
Bold yet shy. Serious yet silly. Chic yet hillbilly.

INDULGE EXTRAVAGANTLY
Sniff out wonderful. Crave what nourishes. Jump in.

SHINE SHYLY
Share your shine selectively. Know when to open up.

THINK ABSTRACTLY
Upside down? Inside out? Metaphysical? No problem.

RELY ON DEXTERITY
Look closely. Solve the puzzle. Unlock the gate.

HIDE WITH FLAIR
Do what you must. Choose their view of you.

BEFRIEND DARKNESS
Shadows are your element. Navigate soul's depths

RHINOCEROS
manifesto

SNIFF
Identify. Delineate. Characterize. Trust.

TRUST YOUR FORM
Impenetrable fortress. Protective. Ancient.

DREAM INTENTLY
Sleep deeply. Tap the beyond. Bring great dreams to life.

NOURISH OFTEN
Seek sustenance for body and soul. Lots.

RELY ON THE PATH
Discover best routes. Reuse. See habits as assets.

ALLOW IRRITATION
Welcome annoyance. Dismiss quickly. Notice preferences.

BE SURE-FOOTED
Know where you're going. Walk softly. Lead.

FAVOR THE FEW
Gather in small clusters. Enjoy parallel solitude.

DISPLAY INCONGRUITY
Express your adorability. Surprise and delight.

FIND YOUR PACE
Trust your evolution. Linger. Or charge ahead.

SEA TURTLE
manifesto

COME ASHORE
Haul out. Rest. Dig in. Create.

YOU'RE ALWAYS HOME
Batten down the hatches and retreat as needed.

FIND THE CURRENT
Feel your way. It's a joy ride. Let the energy take you.

EASY DOES IT
The pace is not a race. Small paddles add up to a glide.

LIVE LIGHTLY
Play. Connect with your pals. Buoyantly amuse.

HERE IS BEST
This is where to be. Exactly now.

DREAM YOUR DESTINATION
Navigate by heart. Hold the vision. Be intention.

DIVE
Fathom the depths. Find solace and new ideas.

STAY CENTERED
Find the steady center and surf the turbulence.

TIME IS IRRELEVANT
Divinity is infinity. Breathe. Sense what's next.

SHARK

manifesto

DEEPEN
To live well. To enjoy. To go home.

AIM WITH INFINITE POTENTIAL
Uniquely qualified to power through. Sheer energy.

BE ABRASIVE
Clear the way. Smooth things out. Polish. Refine.

INVITE CLOSENESS
When it feels right. Sense the energy. Connect with peace.

TEAR IT UP
Break it down. Build it back up. Deconstruct to renew.

TAP ANCIENT ROOTS
Seek guidance from ancestors. Here and in the spirit world.

INSIST ON INDEPENDENCE
Give creations a good start. Then let them go. To thrive.

LOLL
Go belly-up for a bit. Languish. Soak it all in.

INTIMIDATE HONORABLY
Steward your power. Wield wisely. Clear the path for good.

MOTION IS MEDITATION
Stay afloat. Sense your surroundings. Go with grace.

"We must go beyond textbooks, go out into the bypaths and untrodden depths of the wilderness and travel and explore and tell the world the glories of our journey."

John Hope Franklin

SKUNK
manifesto

INFLUENCE ENDURES
Your presence compels. Cause them to pause. Make them think.

ASSUME AN UPRIGHT ATTITUDE
Send a signal. Draw a line in the sand and stand by it.

GRACE ENCHANTS
Know where you're going. Step beautifully and nimbly.

GO QUIETLY AND GENTLY
Be confident. Entice. Beguile. You've got this handled.

FOLLOW A CHAMPION
Learn a new skill. Fall in line behind. Observe carefully.

FORGIVENESS IS PEACE
Let your self off the hook. Resolve distress. Be free.

EXPLORE CONTRAST
Chose one extreme or another. Or go between. Or alternate.

STATE INTENTIONS
Get clear. Say it. Out loud. Disperse and amplify the message.

BATTLES ARE OPTIONAL
Be open and direct. Or retreat. The choice is yours.

COURAGE INVIGORATES
Chose it. When you need to. And play for keeps.

be one.
be one.
be one.
be one.
be one.
be one.
be one.
be one.
be one.
be one.
be one.
be one.
be one.
be one.
be one.
be one.
be one.
be one.
be one.
ᴐe one.
e one.
ꓱ one.
 one.
one.
one.
one.
one.
ᴉe.
ne.
ᴉe.

SNAIL;

— manifesto —

BE ONE WITH HOME
Go within. Or emerge. Withdraw to recharge.

MASTER INVISIBILITY
Sneak under the radar. Conquer the world quietly.

BE AN ARROW OF LOVE
Get close. Aim true. Focus. Receive.

NIGHTTIME IS THE RIGHT TIME
The coast is clear. Adventure while others sleep.

MALLEABLE IS STRONG
Shift with the situation. Sense the next move. Adjust.

BE DIMINUITIVELY MONUMENTAL
Plunge into the world. Dream globally. Be gutsy. Yet small.

MANAGE VULNERABILITY
You say where, when, and with whom. Expose. Retreat.

SHELTER NOURISHMENT
Seek improvement. Accrue carefully. Safeguard your cache.

INVESTIGATE WITH CARE
If the first bite's not tasty, move on. Try again elsewhere.

PROCEED GENTLY
Easy pacing trumps speed. Inches add up. Carry on.

SNAKE
manifesto

GRAB OPPORTUNITY
Open wide now. Digest later.

REINVENT YOURSELF
Shed limitations. Upgrade. Grow.

SEXY IS A FORM OF INTELLIGENCE
Your body knows. Swish. Sense. Enjoy.

QUEST FOR COMFORT
Find shade. Or sun. Honor your needs.

BE INFINITY
Encircle yourself. Journey within.

KNOW YOUR POTENTIAL
Master your coiled energy. It spring-loads you for action.

DASH
Speed can be elegant. Accelerate.

IGNORE THE LINE IN THE SAND.
Erase it as you curve into new territory.

HEAL INSTINCTIVELY
Taste the air. Feel the soul. Use what you know.

STAND ON YOUR OWN
Lift yourself into the air. Rise.

SPIDER
manifesto

CONNECT WITH MAGIC
Follow the thread. Moment by moment.

CAPTURE WHAT'S BEST
Let it come to you. Allow the rest to pass through.

STEER STRAIGHT
Aim directly ahead. Be forward. March right in.

SENSITIVITY SERVES
Listen with your whole self. Confirm. Learn to trust.

DAZZLE
Make the ordinary ethereal. Entice. Captivate.

ENERGY IS INFINITE
Rest. Play. Rest. Play. Rest.

DECEIVE WITH DELICACY
Construct the ephemeral. Float on strength.

DROP OUT OF SIGHT
Get away. Cast off for relief.

REMAIN FREE
Avoid entanglement. Detach with love.

EVERYTHING IS CONNECTED
Work your web.

No. 155   sarah bamford seidelmann m.d. | www.whatthewalrusknows.com

SQUIRREL
manifesto

RELISH RESTLESSNESS
Sprint. Stop a sec. Change direction. Do what feels right.

PLAY ON PURPOSE
Chatter, chase, and goad recruits into your game.

FAVOR DISTRACTION
Jump around. Connect the dots. Create galaxies of stars.

BALANCE WITH POISE
Take your act to new heights. Use fancy footwork.

TWITCH
Stay alert. Notice threats. Send out an alarm.

INVESTIGATE
Explore curiously. Examine. Appreciate. Merge.

BE WIDE-EYED
Look around. Trust what you see. Up, down, all around.

HIGHTAIL IT
Something amiss? Scoot. Scamper. Race away.

GNAW
Crack the nut. Solve the problem. Gain the reward.

STOCK UP
Take stock. Load up. Oh, the luxury of cache.

TIGER
manifesto

SINK INTO YOUR SOLITUDE
You are whole and complete. As is.

REVERE YOUR STRIPES
Warm yourself in your luxurious uniqueness.

DEMAND ROOM TO ROAM
Expand your comfort zone to the far horizons.

CLAIM YOUR VOICE
Roar. Growl. Purr. And know when to be silent.

SLINK
Move with easy grace. Make their jaws drop.

DISAPPEAR FROM VIEW
In a crowd. In a bubble bath. In a split second. In a pinch.

STILL YOUR MIND
Lie low. Become the quiet.

BE THE ARROW
You've got the power. Sprint with intent.

PLAY ROUGH
Tough enough to get the job done. And then some.

ENJOY PLEASURE
Lay your defenses down from time to time. Swim in the river.

TURKEY (WILD)
manifesto

SKEDADDLE
When the energy's all wrong, flee. Return to center safely.

GET IN FRONT
Make your presence known. Be obvious. Demand attention.

ENJOY THE CROWD
Gather for group strength. Merge for mutual benefit.

STRUT
When what you love appears, work it. Free the energy.

DANCE FOR PASSION
Spin. Stomp. Hustle. Jiggle all the bits.

RATTLE AND HUM
Express yourself with percussion. To comfort and enliven.

SHARE SPACE
Coexist harmoniously. Respect your roomies.

FOCUS ON PROCESS
Not outcome. Give now your all. You'll get there.

COLLABORATE
To discover solutions. Delegate. Participate.

MULTIPLY OPTIONS
Seek variations. Invent unlikely, extraordinary combos.

WALRUS
manifesto

ALLOW DESIRE TO CATCH FIRE
Put on a show. Convince. (Safety first.)

BELIEVE IN BOUNTY
You already have it all. And there's more than enough.

LOLLLYGAG IN SHALLOWS
No need to go to deep. Find satisfaction just beneath the surface.

GRAB THAT OFFER
Sniff out opportunity. Embrace the one that sings to you.

UNIQUELY YOU
Uncommon. Unequaled. Unlike any other. Unstoppable.

MUY GRANDE TO THE MAX
Expand beyond limitations. Contain variations and multitudes.

LURCH UNSELFCONSCIOUSLY
Grace is overrated. Go pell-mell. Use short-cuts. Scramble.

PRIORITIZE OUTCOME
Arriving is more important than how you look getting there.

GOAD FOR GOOD
Prod. Prompt. Incite. Yourself. And others of your kind.

GET GREGARIOUS
Hang out in large groups. Snort. Cavort. Replenish.

WHALE
manifesto

INTENSIFY BEAUTY
Aim for profound. Swim in the infinite well.

WATER TEACHES
Ride waves. Open wide for bounty. Find flow.

PARTS ARE WHOLE
All bits connect. Fractal to infinity. Rely on it.

MAKE A SPLASH
Burst forth with new ideas. Bring dreams into the open.

GET MYTHICAL
Swallow it up. Incubate. Cough it out. Tell your story.

PLAY WITH YOUR POD
Sing a collective song. Honor the solo. Harmonize.

GO EASILY
Move softly. You'll get there when you get there.

TUNE THE PRESENT
Music is everywhere all the time. Yet only here now.

EXPRESS CONTRADICTIONS
Shine prismatically. Reflect and refract the all. Weave the web.

EXHALE
Let it all flow out. Inhale automatically. Sense the Tantric shift.

splash. splash. splash. splash. splash. splash. splash. splash. splash. splash. splash. splash. splash. splash. splash. splash. splash. splas. splas. spla. splæ. spl. spl. sp. sp. s. s. s.

WOLF
manifesto

SUPERVISE SUBTLY
Send a strong message. With just a nod. A glance. A nudge.

SPEAK WITH EMPATHY
Infuse your message with affection. Connect via heart.

HIERARCHY HELPS
Who leads? Who follows? Who needs a mentor? Who serves?

TEACH WHAT YOU KNOW
Demonstrate. Give feedback. And take it. Improve together.

ADMIRE THE AMATEUR
Honor innocence and wonder. Be green again. Evergreen.

POINT IT OUT
See something others don't? Tell them. Share guidance.

COOPERATE TO CREATE
Dream big. Mobilize together. Infuse with divine energy.

SEEK FREEDOM
Enjoy space. Choose to cruise.

UNLEASH THE PARTY
Socialize often. A mixer is a fixer.

TROT MEDITATIVELY
Steady pacing over the long haul. Sink into your own stride.

WOLVERINE

manifesto

TENACITY IS TANTAMOUNT
Lead with a certain heart. Strike true. Win with intent.

AIM INVISIBLY
Hide. Sense. Know. Launch.

STAY CONNECTED
Check in with what you love. Nurture links.

HOLD THE VISION
Detach from ordinary reality. Dream large. Don't let go.

DIG DOWN DEEP
To your own source of power. Amplify. Channel the infinite.

GET GROUNDED
In the familiar and the beloved. Unearth the everlasting.

ELUDE
Slip away. Find a hollow. Obscure the trail.

FOCUS FANATICALLY
Track the end point. Adjust the trajectory as needed.

ENDURE
Want it? Stick to it. All the way to the very, very end.

SELF IS PEACE
Your route. Your mastery. Your strength.

No. 162

MORE about SARAH

"She knew things that nobody had ever told her - the words of the trees and the wind."

Zora Neale Hurston

I'm a fourth-generation physician (Board-Certified in Anatomic and Clinical Pathology) hailing from the northern shores of Lake Superior, where I was raised by two rather Bohemian individuals and got to grow up with a sister who's an amazing comedian.

I'm married to Mark Seidelmann, whom I adore for so many reasons. We have four children (all certified Zen masters, naturally) and are so very fortunate to live in Duluth, Minnesota, a gorgeous place steeped in natural beauty and inhabited by many remarkable humans.

I AM SO BLESSED!

I practiced pathology for over a decade with a great group of physicians. In 2010, I took a six-month sabbatical from work because I yearned for deeper personal transformation, the kind (as it turns out) that can only be found in the woods. Rather than returning to pathology after my sabbatical, I took the opportunity I'd been given to share the joy I'd found in nature with others.

I believe I was put here to bring joy, lightness, and play to the process of personal transformation. I now work full-time as a speaker and coach.

I received formal coaching training from the brilliant, hilarious Martha Beck (the coach who writes a monthly article for Oprah's *O Magazine*). I've also had the pleasure and thrill of being on the faculty at Jeannette Maw's Good Vibe University (goodvibeuniversity.com), an online community of amazing people interested in deliberately creating fabulous lives for themselves.

My special interest is in helping others forge a deep and satisfying connection with the Earth, which I believe is one of the most effective ways to manifest a life you love. Connecting with Beasties is one of my favorite ways of connecting with the

Earth. The Beasties help us know that what we've been told is "wrong" with us is actually right.

I enjoy doing one-on-one coaching with a small number of clients who want to inspire the world by unleashing their unique creativity, voice, and strengths. I also do retreats for "Irrepressible Women" (and later maybe men, too!) in beautiful natural places like Hawaii and California – combining surfing, nature, shamanic journeying, and play.

You can find me at my website, FollowYourFeelGood.com where I share my methods for finding ways to feel good, and at SarahSeidelmann.com. I share my love of Beasties and their guidance on a podcast called *Squirrel! Radio – The Magic of Animal Totems* (http://itunes.apple.com/us/podcast/squirrel-radio-magic-animal/id391761473). You can listen to or download episodes for free.

My dear friend Suzi Vandersteen and I co-created a website called JoyJunket.com, where we combine our mutual love of interior design, personal style, and spirit. We've created and posted many videos there and on YouTube to inspire and delight. Making videos is one of my passions. You can find videos on a variety of topics, including Beasties, on the Sarah Seidelmann Channel (www.youtube.com/user/SarahSeidelmann).

RECEIVE MY NEWSLETTER TO FIND OUT WHAT'S HAPPENING!

You're welcome to subscribe to my email list to receive my newsletter every few weeks and find out what's happening. (FollowYourFeelGood.com) If you're interested in coming along on a retreat or in doing coaching with me, please send me an email. I'd love to hear from you! (sarah@followyourfeelgood.com).

I hope you follow your FEEL GOOD … and keep your eyes peeled for Beasties! Love, Sarah

THANK YOU

"If the only prayer you said in your whole life
was, "thank you," that would suffice."

Meister Eckhart

Thanks

To Suzi, who helped me go from hiding in a broom closet to spreading my wings. Before I met her, I had no clue how deeply satisfying and rich a friendship could be. Collaborating with her, *playing* together, and sharing our dreams is one of my life's greatest privileges.

To Mark, who's been a honey badger taking a parallel "road less traveled." I thank Mark for loving me, even though I question *everything*, spray-paint the driveway, rearrange the furniture three times in three months, and tend to say (almost) everything out loud in order to process it. Being with him is *the* best part!

To my Mom, who bravely said to my sister and me, "You can be whatever you want to be when you grow up." We did. And it feels GREAT! Oh and Mom, thank you mucho for being my eagle–eyed proof reader (I.O.U. one case of Diet Coke!)

To my Dad, who was the first person to show me what joy really is, by accepting differences, swimming in the Lester River at the Seven Bridges Road, creating stuff from blocks of wood in the garage after dinner, mentoring fatherless boys who needed help, and always daring to learn and to try something new and interesting.

To my sister, Maria Bamford, who is truly an ambassador of joy. She churns the butter (her metaphor for creative work) every day, and that delicious butter is spread around and enjoyed by whoever's lucky enough to get a pat. That makes me think about crispy French bread ... but I digress.

To George, Katherine, Josephine, and Charlie for reminding me to get off the computer and P L AY! I am, bar none, the luckiest Mom in the world. I'm so thankful for their patience and love.

To Martha Beck and those in her tribe, including me, who've been drawn like moths to her very funny, smart, and loving flame. It's a real luxury to have spent time in her presence soaking up her words, which are interspersed with poetry and silliness. She is sublime.

To Grace Kerina, who gracefully guided me through the sometimes rocky river of book writing and copy editing. I'm hugely grateful for her calming and encouraging presence. Without her I could never have wrapped it all up so neatly.

To Drai ... I've been so fortunate to be placed into the awesome, ligtning-fast, hilarious hands of Drai for the design of this book. She magically got inside my brain to bring the book to life in ways that made me scream with joy when I saw the first sample pages. Drai is more than a consumate professional – she's a sister of freaky, divine feminine energy.

To all the fantastic listeners and callers who showed up at *Squirrel! Radio* and to others who have shared their stories of Beasties with me and helped me learn more and love more – especially Susan Honnell, Kim Ramsey Stromgren, Michelle Cook Hill, Laura English, Jeannette Maw, Annette Pederson, Ann-Marie Stojevich, Maggie Thickens, Mary Morehouse, Kathleen Braddy, Erik Pusch, and Greg Gibbs. Their stories have enriched my life and my work.

gratitude. gratitude. gratitude. gratitude. gratitude. gratitude. gratitude. gratitud. gratitud. gratitud. gratitu. gratitu. gratitu. gratit. gratit. gratit. grati. grati. grati. grat. grat. grat. gra. gra. gre. gr. gr. gr. g. g. g.

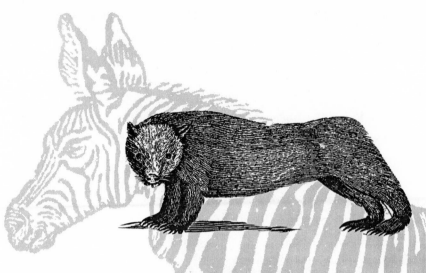

iNDex

" Look at the trees, look at the birds,
look at the clouds, look at the stars...
and if you have eyes, you will be able to
see that the whole existence is joyful. "

Osho

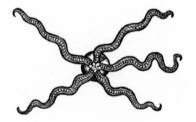

CPSIA information can be obtained at www.ICGtesting.com
Printed in the USA
BVOW041246201111

276508BV00002B/1/P